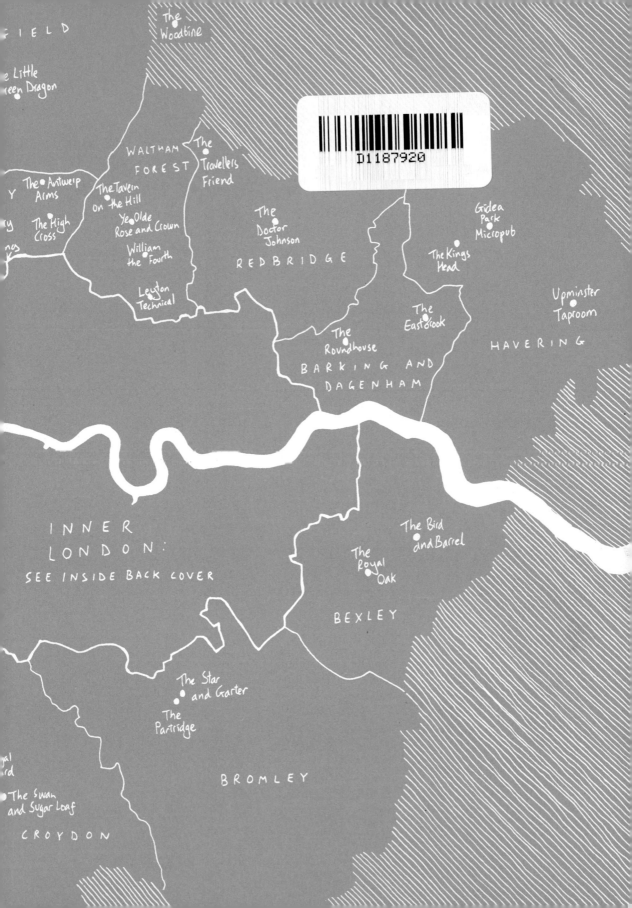

FIELD

The Woodbine

e Little
reen Dragon

WALTHAM

FOREST

The
Travellers
Friend

The Antwerp
Arms

The Tavern
on the Hill

Ye Olde
Rose and Crown

y

The High
Cross

ns

William
the Fourth

Leyton
Technical

The
Doctor
Johnson

REDBRIDGE

Gidea
Park
Micropub

The Kings
Head

Upminster
Taproom

The
Roundhouse

The
Eastbrook

BARKING AND

DAGENHAM

HAVERING

INNER
LONDON:

SEE INSIDE BACK COVER

The Bird
and Barrel

The
Royal
Oak

BEXLEY

The Star
and Garter

The
Partridge

BROMLEY

al
rd

The Swan
and Sugar Loaf

CROYDON

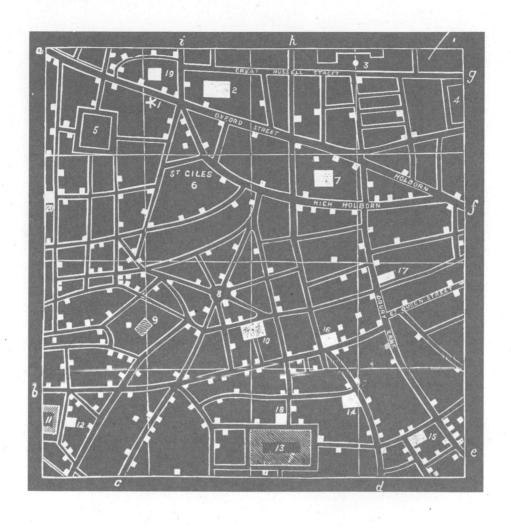

HAPPY BIRTHDAY SAS
THOUGHT THIS BLENDED
A LOT OF OUR INTERESTS
IN ONE FUN BOOK!
THANKS FOR SHARING A
BRAIN WITH ME ♡
LOVE
    RACH x

2023

Previous: *One Half-mile Square in the Heart of London*, 1878. The small squares represent public houses. Courtesy British Library

Above: *A night walk round central London*, 1957.
© John Deakin / John Deakin Archive / Bridgeman Images

Public House

A cultural and social history
of the London pub

Edited by David Knight
and Cristina Monteiro

Open City

Preface
Sadiq Khan,
Mayor of London

London's pubs are without doubt the best in the world. They're an intrinsic part of our city's communities, culture and heritage, and over the years have mirrored the great societal and political shifts in the capital.

But London's pubs don't just reflect our history, they've also shaped the lives of Londoners too. Pubs are places where we've met new friends and partners, where we've discovered new music and been entertained, and where we've come together around a common interest, whether that's live performance, food, football, or a traditional pub quiz. London's pubs have played a crucial role as meeting points for exiled members of the French Resistance during the first world war, the LGBTQ+ community battling for equal rights, and black community leaders fighting for racial justice.

But despite the rich history and diversity of London's pubs, there's no doubt that the last few years have been incredibly challenging. Until 2016 the capital lost far too many pubs, so as Mayor I changed the planning rules to protect our pubs, making it much harder for them to be closed or redeveloped. More recently, pubs were forced to shut their doors due to Covid, putting an unprecedented strain on so many of our cherished venues.

That's why I've taken steps to put our world-class pubs, restaurants and hospitality venues at the heart of London's recovery, launching the biggest domestic tourism campaign our city has ever seen. *LetsDoLondon* is a direct call to Londoners and to the millions of people who visit our city every year to go out and enjoy our amazing pubs and cultural venues. As we seek to bounce back from this crisis, it is more important than ever to support the staff and workers who keep our pubs vibrant, welcoming and open around the clock.

Pubs will continue to play a key role in our capital's communities and social fabric. But we can't take their future for granted – we must all play our part in ensuring their survival. As much as London's fascinating and vivid history can be told through the life of our pubs, life in London will be all the richer if we can preserve our precious pubs for generations to come.

A carved limestone pub sign dating from the rebuilding of London after the Great Fire of 1667. © Museum of London

Foreword
David Knight
Cristina Monteiro

For two decades London's pubs have been central to our lives.
In them we have celebrated and recovered, forged lasting
friendships, danced to unforgettable gigs, met with clients
and members of the public as part of our professional lives,
taught, lectured, argued (among ourselves and with others),
discovered new perspectives, led workshops, marked birthdays,
and found ways of navigating the city. London's pubs have
brought us into contact with people who share similar
obsessions and enthusiasms, and with those who are so
different from us that striking up a friendship in any other
context is hard to imagine.

When not editing this book, we are part of DK-CM, an
architecture and planning practice which primarily works
with and for the public; designing public buildings, public
spaces, and also public documents such as spatial policy
and design guides. We are interested in the ways that places
change – in the role of people in creating that change, and
in how we can make a built environment that offers more to
current and future generations. The lessons of the pub come
up repeatedly in our working lives: the importance of places
that allow for divergent thinking and for breaking out of siloed
echo chambers; how spaces can thrive through a collective
sense of ownership; how to make buildings that age well

and allow for adaptation; the value of places which combine
a sense of publicness with a sense of homeliness.

Ten years ago we were involved in teaching on the architecture
programme at Kingston University School of Art. With our fellow
tutors, we set out to document London's pubs, firstly to explore
the lessons they might have for how we design a shared or collective building in contemporary London, and secondly to consider
how we might protect pubs from the forces of development that
play such a huge role in pub closures. We explored the intangible
qualities and practices that make the pub special and how these
relate to questions of architecture and design. The extraordinary
drawings of London pubs that appear in this book were made
for that project. We hope they, along with the many artefacts,
photographs and illustrations also included, capture the people
and architecture that, in various ways, always come together
to make a potent pub. More broadly, we also believe that they
point to a better future London with a more complex, generous
social infrastructure.

During the development of this book we conducted Zoom
calls with the authors whose writing appears here sharing
one-minute Lumière films made by those Kingston students
ten years ago (the nearest we could get to being in a London pub
during Covid). We saw in those videos people using the pub as
a place to meet, share, drink, think, to be together or comfortably
alone in a space that somehow exists between the public realm
of the street and the private realm of the home. Watching those
films, we realised over and over how much we missed this sense
of a shared interior – of being close together in a room, of
participating in the collective life of our community and our city.

The 121 pubs in *Public House* each have a story to tell about
the complex role of the pub in London. They are arranged
chronologically, with the dating chosen not from when the pub
opened but from when it had the most interesting story to tell.
Most of the stories are described in short vignettes written by
ourselves, but 15 of them have been the triggers for longer and
more in-depth exploration in essays by a variety of contributors –
among them musicians, architects, journalists, comedians,
politicians and artists. To help frame this extraordinarily twisty
tale, an essay-length introduction charts the various evolutions

of the London pub. Though the book is emphatically not a guide to the 'best' pubs of the city, or the 'best places to buy a pint', many of the pubs that meet those criteria are included here as part of a richer journey. While *Public House* can be read chronologically, as a history, like all good pub conversations, it also allows the reader to meander, following references across the book and across time to trace new connections and new meanings.

We have tried to make a book which celebrates the pub whilst also bringing critical perspectives to bear on it, with the ultimate intention of better understanding its role in a London which is rapidly changing. This is especially urgent in a context where the protection of what's good and vital about our built environment, and a progressive approach to its renewal, both feel under threat. The pub reminds us that one of the most important things about a city is its complexity and diversity. There are no easy answers or formulas for London's future, but we believe in looking to the city's intricacies and differences in order to develop strategies that are socially and environmentally sound, and which look and feel like London.

Pubs are closing every day in London and the UK, and this has been exacerbated by the pandemic. It is currently extraordinarily easy, with the right capital, to shift a pub into a small supermarket or into private dwellings, or to reduce it to a ground-level retail unit surrounded by other development. This reflects the fact that our planning system makes it relatively easy to protect the fabric of an architecturally significant pub building, but we have little power to protect or support its social and cultural significance. The stones remain but the pub has gone. This book celebrates the special architecture of the pub, but it also celebrates the practices, codes, behaviours, memories, customs and stories that are today very easily swept away. We hope it will contribute to a better, more open conversation about what a pub is and how it is valued and protected.

Sometimes pub closures are not much mourned, or their loss is hard to read. But more often than not there are protests, collective sorrow, ongoing battles and campaigns. The threatened closure of a pub can, if the counterattack wins out, lead to a rejuvenated pub and a rejuvenated community.

In parallel to the closures and sell-offs, a remarkable ground-swell in activity and enthusiasm for pubs is also taking place. Crowdfunding campaigns across society have mobilised to protect or support beloved locals, and in many cases have flipped established pubs into more community-focused, atmospheric and lively places. Craft and independent brewers are starting to run, refurbish and even build pubs, and to do so in ways that respond to pub traditions but also create new kinds of pub that are more inclusive and diverse. Though central London is lagging behind due to high land values, Micropubs and Community-owned pubs are now appearing everywhere on the city's outskirts, representing significant challenges to conventional ideas of how pubs are run. In a context of declining numbers, the world of the public house is also entering an exciting new period in its history. This book is a celebration of that moment, as well as of the pub's longer story.

Like a good pub at the right time of day, the voices in this book are sometimes serious, sometimes playful. Strident arguments intermingle with gentle stories, speaking to each other and across centuries. Also like a good pub, the book has been designed to be durable, a little grand, but not intrusively so. The idea is really all about bringing some interesting and very different voices together, and in doing so, we hope, making the case for the cultural, social and architectural value of the public house to our city and our society.

Introduction 12

David Knight

The George Inn, Southwark   26
The Queens Head, Harrow   26
Ye Olde Cheshire Cheese,
   City of London   27
The Seven Stars, Camden   30
The Jamaica Wine House, City of London   32
The Spotted Dog, Newham   32
The White Swan, Richmond   33
The Plume of Feathers, Greenwich   33
Ye Olde Mitre, Camden   34
The Spaniards, Barnet   36
The White Raven, Tower Hamlets*   36
The Grenadier, Westminster   37
The Anglesea Arms,
   Kensington and Chelsea   37
The Oddfellows Arms, Harrow   38
The Sutton Arms, Islington   38
The Case is Altered, Hillingdon   39
The Three Crowns, Hackney   39
The Queen's Arms,
   Kensington and Chelsea   39
The Royal Oak, Bexley   40
The Trafalgar Tavern, Greenwich   40

The Blue Posts 42

Laura C. Forster

The Tabard, Hounslow   47
The Royal Oak, Brent   47
The Kings Head, Wandsworth   48
The Swan and Sugarloaf, Croydon   48
The Star and Garter, Bromley   49
The Viaduct Tavern, City of London   49
The Fox and Anchor, Islington   52
The Salisbury, Haringey   54
The Castle Inn, Harrow   55
The Fox, Enfield   55
The Boleyn, Newham   56
The Blackfriar, City of London   56
The Brewery Tap, Hounslow   57
The Trafalgar Freehouse, Hounslow   57
The Lord Clyde, Southwark   58

King Edward VII, Newham   58
The Cock, Sutton*   59

The Mothers Arms 60

Clare Cumberlidge, Ruth Ewan

The Fitzroy Tavern, Camden   67
Cittie of Yorke, Camden   70
The Duke's Head, Wandsworth   70

The Fellowship 72

Jessica Boak, Ray Bailey

The Angel, Hillingdon*   77
The Black Lion,
   Hammersmith and Fulham   77
The Atlas, Kensington and Chelsea   80
The Ace of Spades, Kingston   80

The Earl Beatty 82

Neal Shasore

The Eastbrook, Barking and Dagenham   90
The Windermere, Brent   92
The Doctor Johnson, Redbridge*   92
The Palm Tree, Tower Hamlets   93
Skehans, Lewisham   93
The Travellers Friend, Redbridge   94
The Bride of Denmark, Westminster*   94

The City of Quebec 98

Paul Flynn

The White Hart, Hillingdon   102
The French House, Westminster   102
The Kenilworth Castle,
   Kensington and Chelsea*   104
The Lord Nelson, Southwark   106
The Shakespeare's Head, Islington   107
The Cavendish Arms, Lambeth   107
The Willoughby Arms, Kingston   108
The Coach and Horses, Lambeth   108
The Barley Mow, Westminster   109
The Kings Head, Havering*   109
The Roundhouse, Barking and Dagenham   112
The Royal Standard, Croydon   113

The Hole in the Wall, Lambeth   113
The Hope and Anchor, Islington   114
The Golden Heart, Tower Hamlets   114
The Atlantic, Lambeth   116
The Bedford Hotel, Wandsworth   117
The Pride of Spitalfields,
    Tower Hamlets   117

The Queen Victoria   118

Rupa Huq

The Wenlock Arms, Hackney   122
The Partridge, Bromley   124
The Windmill, Lambeth   125
The Harp, Westminster   125
The Grapes, Tower Hamlets   126

The Jerusalem Tavern   128

Phineas Harper, David Knight, Cristina Monteiro, Daniel Rosbottom, Bernd Schmutz, Timothy Smith, Eleanor Suess, Jonathan Taylor

The Royal Oak, Southwark   136
The Foundry, Hackney*   136
The Golden Anchor, Southwark   140
The Social, Westminster   140
William the Fourth, Waltham Forest   141
The Glass Bar, Camden*   141
Ye Olde Rose and Crown, Waltham Forest 142
The Eagle, Lambeth   142
The Prince of Wales, Ealing   143
The Masons Arms, Richmond   143

The Albany   146

Isy Suttie

The Southampton Arms, Camden   151
The Old Orchard, Hillingdon   151

The Woodbine Inn   154

Luke Turner

The Betsey Trotwood   158

Bob Stanley

The Anchor and Hope   164

Jennifer Lucy Allan

The Hope, Sutton   168
The Leyton Technical,
    Waltham Forest   168
The Cock Tavern, Hackney   169
The Faltering Fullback, Haringey   169
The Chandos Arms, Barnet   169

The Joiners Arms   170

Lily Waite

The Glory, Hackney   174
Upminster Tap Room, Havering   175
The African Queen, Hounslow   175

The Antwerp Arms   176

Jonathan Moses

The Marksman, Tower Hamlets   180
The Queen Adelaide, Hackney   180
The Royal Vauxhall Tavern, Lambeth   181

The Hare   184

Orit Gat

The Lord Napier, Tower Hamlets   190
The Dodo Micropub, Ealing   190
Gidea Park Micropub, Havering   191
The Prince of Peckham, Southwark   191
The Bill Murray, Islington   192
The Little Green Dragon, Enfield   192
The Bird and Barrel, Bexley   193
The High Cross, Haringey   193

Tavern on the Hill   194

Nana Biamah Ofosu, Jaega Wise

The Carlton Tavern, Westminster   199

Texts written by the editors unless otherwise stated.
Pubs with an * are not trading at the time of writing.

Introduction
David Knight

Greater London spans over 600 square miles including in its boundaries many public houses that would not for decades or centuries have considered themselves London pubs at all. But, thanks to London's scale, complexity and significance, the city has England's greatest concentration and diversity of public houses.

If there is a single origin to the public house, it's the moment when a domestic space is opened up to the public in order to sell them a drink; a convivial blurring of the private and public spheres. The pub has since experienced extraordinary transformation and reimagination – reflecting, and sometimes shaping, wider social and cultural changes. Pub types have merged, disappeared, hybridised, evolved, rebooted and generally got incredibly and delightfully confused over the centuries.

What is now known as 'the pub' developed out of various distinct types which would not have fallen under a single banner in their time: the Alehouse, the Coaching Inn, the Tavern and the Coffee House. They've mutated so much over the years, and their names have been used so interchangeably, that the distinctions can feel impossible to unpick, but here goes.

The Alehouse was an ordinary home modified to serve ale to the public. From the Norman Conquest to the English civil war Alehouses were heavily legislated and licensed, which often

encouraged the subtlety (or even invisibility) of their appearance; signage was non-existent, occasionally just a painted key-stone above a door. Some historical accounts describe the Alehouse as a temporal space – a sign would be periodically hung outside an otherwise ordinary dwelling once beer had been brewed. Contrary to ideas of the pub as a traditionally male domain, the ale of a pre-industrialisation Alehouse would typically be brewed by the women of the home, giving rise to the term 'alewife' (The Mothers Arms, p60). As early as the 14th century, many single and widowed women were using brewing to carve out independent livelihoods running Alehouses.

The Inn is similarly ancient with surviving examples dating from the 12th and 13th centuries. Inns provided lodgings, food, drink and related services as part of a nationwide transportation network of horse-drawn carriages. Some were almost settlements in their own right, sitting at key moments of interchange or along pilgrimage routes. Others clustered together in existing cities and market towns, as termini from which the benefits of urban life – trade, politics, society – could be had. For this reason London had the richest concentration in the country: a dense ring of Inns surrounding the City of London, Southwark and Whitehall with more dotted along the roads out into the countryside, and clustered at the key junctions and chartered market towns that today form nodes of Greater London. In important market locations like Romford and Southwark, Inns were built side-by-side, competing directly for business and taking on distinct characters and reputations as a result. These were not places aimed at a regular local community but instead provided a sense of place and homeliness to diverse travellers, sometimes enriched by sporting events, political activity, sitting courts and theatre.

Inns were often multi-storeyed buildings framing yards for stabling, sometimes with upstairs rooms accessed by external galleries which could be used as performance spaces. Across the centuries the style of Inns varied from informal timber-framed or other vernacular forms of construction through to elaborate classically-inflected edifices. Inns were also notable for their large, bespoke signs that communicated the name of the establishment in a visual language that could be understood by all – whether literate or not. In urban areas Inn signs often stretched into the middle of the street or arched all the way across. While London's Inns have mostly been destroyed, the George (p26) is a unique survivor of the

Above: Mother Louse, Oxfordshire alewife, 1880s. Courtesy Wellcome Collection

Below: Illustration of an inn, 1337 – the diagonal cross over the doorway is a reference to crossroads.

galleried terminus type and the Spaniards (p36) is a surviving roadside example, complete with an 18th century toll booth.

The Tavern is a third distinct type evolving primarily to serve imported wine under more strict licensing and taxation. With regulation came legitimacy so Taverns could declare themselves more confidently than Alehouses, and the rich history of typography, signage and graphics associated with pubs (other than Inn signs) developed from here. Thanks to their more prestigious and exotic product, Taverns were frequented by well-off clients who used them as restaurants and meeting rooms (and sometimes brothels). The origin of the word 'tavern' is Latin, perhaps suggesting a tangible link to the Roman Empire's practice of transporting wine across its territories. Until the 17th century, London's excise office, which managed Tavern licensing, was based on a small yard off Fleet Street adjacent – surely not by coincidence – to a pub that provides perhaps the closest atmosphere contemporary London can offer to that of a real Tavern, Ye Olde Cheshire Cheese (p27).

The Coffee House emerged in the mid-17th century, swiftly following the arrival of coffee itself to England. The Jamaica Wine House (p32) was one of the first to be built in London but the type spread, becoming a powerful institution. They were widely known as centres of debate and political discourse partly because, as the day wore on, their clientele grew caffeinated rather than drunk. Coffee Houses often used imagery and names based on an orientalist understanding of coffee-growing nations. In time, many lost their focus on coffee and their role began to blur with more established types of pub, but in the City of London their significance continued. Institutions known today as some of the most powerful in the city have their origins in Coffee Houses, most famously the insurance market, Lloyd's of London.

Over the decades Alehouses, Inns, Taverns and Coffee Houses have mixed and blurred, spawning many hybrids. By the 18th and 19th centuries few establishments would have been pure versions of any one type and the term 'public house' was used to describe all four and everything in between, as political events continued to drive new mutations in pub design.

Since the mid-18th century official anxiety had been growing about the social impact of spirit consumption, particularly gin. The resulting 1830 Beerhouse Act aimed to curb gin consumption by liberalising the brewing and sale of beer,

Above: Carved wooden inn sign of the Peterboat and Double Tavern, Fish Street Hill, 1600s. © Edwin Smith / RIBA Collections

Opposite: Ye Olde Cheshire Cheese, 145 Fleet Street

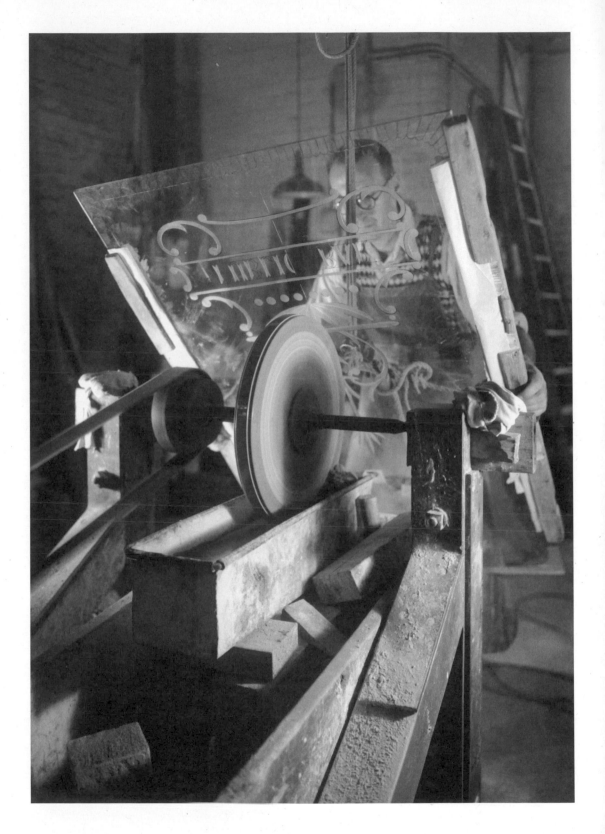

leading almost overnight to an explosion of Beerhouses; most of them simple, domestic interiors unselfconsciously adapted for customers. By 1838 there was a pub for every 186 people, around eight times more pubs per capita than today. The Oddfellows Arms (p38) is likely to have begun life in this way, and the feeling of this type of domestic-scale pub is also approximated in Ye Olde Mitre (p34).

As independent Beerhouses boomed, breweries were taking on a stronger role in the design and management of pubs. The 'Tied House system', also known as the 'London system' because it was pioneered by London's large commercial breweries, involved breweries buying up pubs and then leasing them out on the condition that their tenants sold the brewery's beers. The Tied House led to an explosion of commercial graphics and signage through which the parent brewery's brand often overwhelmed the identity of the individual pub. A late example can be seen at the Lord Clyde (p58), but photos of the 19th century city typically show pubs adorned from cornice to foundations in bold brewery signage. Under the control of breweries, pub architecture became increasingly standardised but more ambitious in formal terms, with in-house architects employed by breweries to create elaborate buildings with proprietary furniture and signage to be rolled out across their estates. Many of these brewery architects held their roles for years, developing methods of achieving local distinction within the efficiencies of standardisation.

With Beerhouses proliferating, the more heavily-licensed houses that sold gin and spirits began to create a distinctive architectural language in response. They became known as Gin Palaces and were notable for their palatial, opulent and complex interiors, including highly-wrought timberwork often using classical forms and imagery. Cut glass, glazed tiles, textured ceilings, and elaborate screens of various types for subdividing the interior by class and by price abounded. The Viaduct Tavern (p49) and the Boleyn (p56) are both significant examples of this protracted Victorian moment when the image of the urban pub really solidified. The bar as a nexus around which the pub is organised also dates from this time, and in the Gin Palace it becomes something architecturally sumptuous and formally adventurous. Again, with time, the boundaries between types blurred, and we now can't find a single Gin Palace that won't also serve a pint.

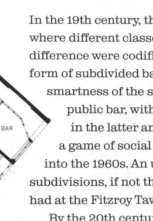

In the 19th century, the public house became a place not only where different classes mixed but where class anxiety and difference were codified; given architectural expression in the form of subdivided bars for different segments of society. The smartness of the saloon was set against the austerity of the public bar, with billiards in the former and bar-billiards in the latter and different prices for the same drink in a game of social stratification that remained in some pubs into the 1960s. An understanding of the architecture of these subdivisions, if not the class prejudices they embodied, can be had at the Fitzroy Tavern (p67).

By the 20th century, multiple spaces for particular uses were commonplace in pubs, among them function rooms, billiard halls, basement bars, even large rooms for theatre or music hall, plus a cellar used to store and cool the drinks. This expansion of facilities intensified between the first and second world wars, with a huge growth in the delivery of public and private housing. Many of the planners and architects of this new housing had been schooled in the Arts and Crafts and Garden City Movement which – alongside its advocacy of settlements that combined 'the best of town and country' – was notable for its alignment with Temperance, an ideology opposing the consumption of alcohol. In this context many new developments, in marked contrast to the Georgian expansion of the city, lacked new pubs or severely limited their construction. Meanwhile, the government, also keen to promote sobriety, had since 1916 been experimenting with national-ising brewing and pub management in Carlisle, Enfield and Cromarty Firth. In response to their critics, breweries began investing in pubs with a wider offer of facilities aiming to appeal to women and to families, and including dedicated spaces for outdoor drinking and dining, entertainment and games. The Fellowship (p72) and the Angel (p77) are both early examples of the type, which became known as Improved Pubs and which in the early days tended toward established architectural languages echoing Georgian or Tudor aesthetics, consciously avoiding the lavishness of the Gin Palace. Later, the Improved Pub would – in tandem with suburban architecture more gen-erally – expand to include Modernist architectural vocabulary too and become significantly more eclectic. Examples of this latter period include the Windermere (p92), the Roundhouse (p112), the Doctor Johnson (p92) and the Earl Beatty (p82), all built near significant new interwar housing developments.

Above: Ground floor of the Union Tavern, Camberwell, 1897 – designed by William Brutton who was also responsible for the Fitzroy Tavern.

Opposite: Devonshire Arms, Marylebone, 1888 (photo taken by Sam Lambert, 1960). © Architectural Press Archive / RIBA Collections

19

The explosion in car ownership amid the early 20th century and influence of US precedents led to a variation on the Improved Pub appearing alongside new bypasses and ringroads: Roadhouses. These were supercharged, sprawling places featuring full-scale dancehalls and swimming pools. In London, no Roadhouses survive in anything like their original form but some linger on as service stations or garages, often with the original architecture all but lost, for example at the Ace of Spades (p80).

During the second world war the idea of state-led planning, including government-backed construction and laws constraining metropolitan sprawl, became mainstream and an extraordinarily ambitious and confident wave of urban redevelopment arrived with the outbreak of peace. This was the period of limiting London's growth (through the creation of the Green Belt), redistributing its populations to orbital communities (through the creation of the New Towns) and even redefining London's political and geographic boundaries (through the founding of the Greater London Council). Postwar Pubs built in the new communities of this extraordinary period took on its brave new aesthetics, often combined with more archaic forms referencing nautical, royal or historical motifs. The Lord Nelson (p106), the Shakespeare's Head (p107), the Cavendish Arms (p107) and the Windmill (p125) are all surviving examples of the type,

Above: Illustration of a small public bar by John Ambrose and Jeffrey Lyde, c.1950

Opposite: Extension to the Wargrave Arms public house, 42 Brendon Street, Marylebone, 1961 © Henk Snoek / RIBA Collections

though the New Towns around London are home to many more. Brits seem to always treat the architecture of their recent past with contempt and so most Postwar Pubs have today been radically altered or demolished, just as many Victorian pubs were lost before them.

The public house has always been rooted in a rich variety of types, but across the 20th century fragmented into an even greater diversity in response to particular local needs, cultures, genders and demographics. Pubs specifically catering for LGBTQ+ communities have always existed in spite of repression. London's 1930s bohemian venues drew diverse queer and black revellers but, tellingly, some of the only surviving plans are from police raids. It was only in the late-20th century with civil rights breakthroughs that queer culture became openly reflected in the character of the pub. The Royal Vauxhall Tavern (p181) was noted for at least one of its bars serving a gay crowd well in advance of the 1967 decriminalisation of homosexuality, and today London has a rich diversity of LGBTQ+ pubs. Examples include the City of Quebec (p98), the Queen Adelaide (p180) and the Glory (p174), though the now-lost Glass Bar (p141) stood as a shamefully rare example of a space for lesbians.

Pubs run by and for black and brown Londoners also have a long history often under-reflected in the physical character of buildings themselves. It is only in comparatively recent examples such as the Golden Anchor (p140) where aesthetic references of meaning to the black community now play a strong role in the place. The story of George Berry, landlord of the Coach and Horses (p108) and London's first black pub owner speaks to a larger and richer narrative of black publicans than is normally recognised.

In the 1960s and 1970s, in reaction to the industrialised beer of the big English breweries and imported lagers, organisations like the Campaign for Real Ale (CAMRA) and the Society for the Preservation of Beers from the Wood were founded, initially calling for better beer but soon campaigning for better pubs to drink it in too. CAMRA's definition of real ale was limited to cask ales that could only really be served at a pub bar, adding an inherently architectural dimension to their cause. The ensuing rise of pubs broadly delivering to the specifications of CAMRA were often Freehouses, untethered from any particular brewery so able to hand-pick the range of beers they sold. The word 'Boozer' has been used to describe

Police sketch plan of Billie's Club, 6 Little Denmark Street, Soho, 1936. Courtesy National Archives

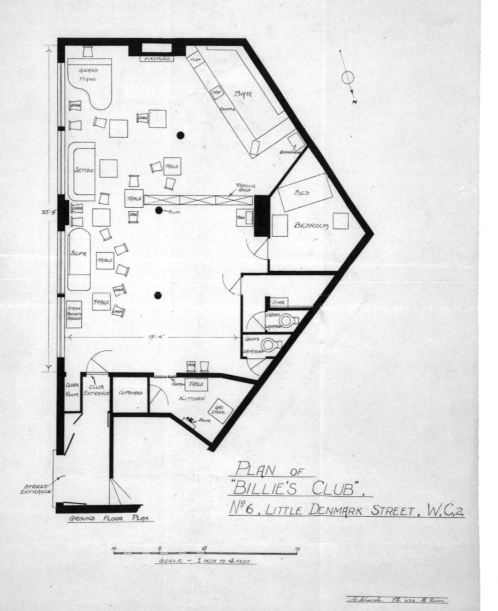

GRAND PIANO

FIREPLACE

FLAP

CHAIR

BAR

COUNTER

CHAIR

SETTEE

TABLE

TABLE

CHAIR

TRELLIS ARCH

GARNISHINGS

BED

BEDROOM

35'-9"

SOFA

TABLE

TABLE

CHAIR

STAGE PROPERTY BASKET

TABLE

CHAIR

19'-4"

SINK

LADIES LAVATORY

GENTS LAVATORY

CLOAK ROOM

CLUB ENTRANCE

CUPBOARD

CURTAIN

TABLE

KITCHEN

GAS STOVE

PHONE

STREET ENTRANCE

GROUND FLOOR PLAN

PLAN OF
"BILLIE'S CLUB",
Nº 6, LITTLE DENMARK STREET, W.C.2.

10   5   0   10

SCALE - 2 INCH TO 4 FEET

pubs for a long time (I can't find its exact origin) but today the term is used almost interchangeably with these real ale-prioritising pubs. Examples include the Anglesea Arms (p37), the Sutton Arms (p38), the Barley Mow (p109), the Masons Arms (p143), the Pride of Spitalfields (p177) and the Wenlock Arms (p123).

The ascent of the Boozer has gone hand-in-hand with the proliferation of Gastropubs, public houses serving food to the point of flirting with the feel and style of restaurants; notable chefs often taking on management roles as well as culinary ones. The Eagle on Farringdon Road was a pioneer, and other examples include the Seven Stars (p31) and the Marksman (p180). The Gastropub movement has been so influential that, combined with reduced social drinking, it has pervaded almost the entire pub industry, with a dwindling number of pubs not selling any freshly-cooked food at all. The Desi Pub, typically run by South Asian landlords, combines Boozer-ish spaces with South Asian foods such as the karahi grill, and are often found in areas with a large-enough population of diasporic people to sustain the business. The Prince of Wales (p143) and the African Queen (p175) are notable examples.

A lot has been written on the adverse impact of the smoking ban, supermarket beer and land values on pubs. Apart from wider narratives of decline and closure, these forces have nonetheless catalysed two creative responses among London's pubs; Community Pubs and Micropubs. A rising tide of well-organised communities have increasingly refused to accept the claims of large breweries and property developers that treasured existing pubs were unviable, and have taken control and ownership themselves. Reflecting the enormous impact of property values on London as a whole, successful examples of this pub type tend to be more prominent in outer London, such as the Hope (p168) and the Antwerp Arms (p176). The term Community Pub is also often used to describe pubs not under community ownership but those which feel like they are, in that they play a larger than usual role in the life of their neighbourhood; examples include the Trafalgar Freehouse (p57) and the Masons Arms (p143).

The Micropub is another response to the challenges of the present and is the final pub type in this guide. After all the twists and turns of this story, it brings us back not only to the simple Beerhouse of the 1830s but also to the medieval Alehouse where we began: Micropubs are small, rigorously

Above: Campaign for Real Ale (CAMRA) button badge c.1975

Opposite: Drawing of the author by Amelia Monteiro Knight, 2021.

independent and tend to be run in a very personal manner by an individual, couple or family with an aesthetic that is simple and unselfconscious. They have frequently appeared in former high street buildings rather than homes, and architecturally are hard to distinguish from the rest of a run of shops. Generally lacking a cellar, they often use cooled back rooms from which to dispense the beer in another call-back to more ancient models. Similar to the Community Pub, the Micropub is for now a chiefly a suburban or Outer London condition, as can be seen in some excellent examples: the Upminster Tap Room (p175), the Dodo Micropub (p190), and the Little Green Dragon (p192), the last of which is a particularly vivid example as it replaced a large Improved Pub lost to a supermarket. As the character of London changes in the wake of the pandemic, high streets and town centres are hollowing out, shifting to residential uses where once there were shops and restaurants. Might Micropubs and Alehouses be able to carve out space in future metropolitan centres? In Haringey, the council have recently supported the transformation of a former public toilet on Tottenham High Road into a new pub (p193). A pub, albeit an unusual one, is once again the most prominent and public part of this stretch of the city.

Transformation and reimagination are fundamental to the history of the pub. Changing constantly whilst remaining true to a certain collectively-established sense of itself, the pub often manages to feel timeless while in a permanent state of shifting evolution. This balance of change and continuity is fundamental to the pub's appeal, continuing today as pubs rework their offer, buildings and landscapes in response to the pandemic. Pubs will continue to reflect and support social change – sometimes in ordinary ways, sometimes in extraordinary ways. Every pub in this book is part of that story.

The Queens Head

Harrow, HA5 5PJ

An architectural puzzle, the Queens Head is both an Inn dating from the 16th century and a 20th century invention; both Tudor and Mock-Tudor. Originally a private house built on the high street of Pinner village in around 1536, it was extensively renovated and reworked (retaining a large proportion of the 16th century timber frame) in 1929. Around this time, Pinner was rapidly transforming from Middlesex village to London suburb. Mock-Tudor was emerging as the favoured style of the interwar suburb, based loosely on half-timbered originals and the Arts and Crafts movement, so that a drink in the Queens Head today is a chance to explore not only a Tudor rural Inn but also the interwar dream of the semi-rural pastoral suburb.

1388

The George Inn

Southwark, SE1 1NH

London was once the centre of a vast network of Inns built in cities, market towns and at strategic locations along the country's road network. Inns served as termini for stagecoach operators providing horse-drawn transport across the country, offering lodgings for visitors to the city, and rooms for political groups, informal courts and business. The George was one of a large number of these galleried Inns in London but today is the only survivor. Sitting amid the still-convivial courtyard in the shadow of its galleries today, we're in a mainly 17th century creation. The northern range is long gone, but the Inn is medieval in origin and was a going concern in 1388 when Chaucer's pilgrims set off for Canterbury from the Tabard Inn just next door.

Queens Head **Pinner**

CZECHOSLOVAKIAN MATCHES

© BOULDENS MATCHES Tel: 0489 583911

1538

Ye Olde Cheshire Cheese

City of London, EC4A 2BU

In the 16th century only a Tavern could sell wine for consumption on the premises, and the number of licenses available was tightly regulated. The Excise Office that did the regulating was based at Wine Office Court, but go there today and you'll instead find Ye Olde Cheshire Cheese, the closest thing we have to one of those 16th century Taverns: all dark-panelled rooms, creaky staircases and open fires. The Cheese and the Excise Office were neighbours in the 16th century, but the pub was rebuilt after the Great Fire of 1666 and much of what we lurk in now is significantly newer (though there are claims that the brilliantly cavernous basement bar was once part of an ancient monastery). Sexually explicit ceramic tiles were found after a fire in the 1960s, strongly hinting that the Cheese's upstairs rooms served as a brothel in the 18th century.

Right and overleaf: New York Public Library

Soup.

Real Turtle = = = = = 2/6

Clear or Tomato *6*

Fish.

Dover Sole (Grilled or Fried) = = =

Salmon Mayonnaise

The Dish of the Day.

12.30

Ye famous Pigeon Pie *2/-*

Cold Sirloin Beef

Shepherds Pie

6.30

Ye famous Pigeon Pie *2/-*

R. Grouse, Bread Sauce & Chips

Cold Dishes.

R. Grouse *1/9* *Duck & Apple Sauce*

Tongue & Ham *1/6* *Chicken & Ham*

Roast Beef

The "BOOK OF THE CHEESE" 1/- per Copy.   For Prices of SOU

Cellars full of Rare
Schweppes Sod

To=day.

From "Ye Olde Grylle."

			Steak	-	-	-	1/2
Chop- - - -	1/-		Steak - - -	1/2
Kidney - - -	6d.		Point Steak -	1/4
York Ham - -	1/6		Fillet Steak- -	1/4
Sausage - - -	3d.		Two Cutlets -	1/-
Two Sausages on			Tomatoes - -	6d.
Brown Mash -	9d.		Mushrooms - -	6d.

Vegetables.

			Fried Onions - -	4d.
Potatoes (Boiled) -	2d.		Fried Onions - -	4d.
Do. (Baked) -	2d.		
Do. (Mashed) -	3d.		

Sweets.

Ye Pancake - 6d.

Ye Toasted Cheese - - = - 6d.

Cheshire (White or Red)	2d.
Bread - - -	1d.
Butter - - -	1d.
Cream - - -	2d.
	Per Cup.
Coffee & Hot Milk (large)	6d.
Do. do. (small)	4d.
Black Coffee - -	4d.

Marston's
Pale
and
Burton
Ales
on
Draught
here.

d POSTCARD VIEWS OF THE HOUSE, *see Page 15 of* WINE LIST.

nes. See Wine List.

Ginger Ale, etc.

The Seven Stars

THE
WIG
BOX

WINES & SPIRITS

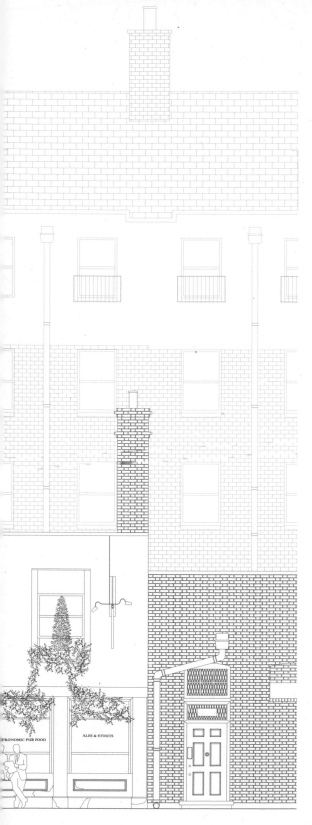

1602

The Seven Stars

Camden, WC2A 2JB

The Seven Stars has existed for centuries –
its signboard says 1602 – and it was originally
built as part of the mews development behind
New Square, Lincoln's Inn. As a result, it is
extremely shallow with more space behind
the bar than in front of it and the otherwise
quiet central London backstreet becoming
the real front of house. Roxy Beaujolais took
over the Seven Stars in 2001 having previously run the Three Greyhounds in Soho
and authored *Home from the Inn Contented*
(1996), a definitive pre-gastropub cookbook.
The interior was very beautifully redesigned –
in a way that makes it look very much not-
designed while evoking the pub's long
history – by Roxy's husband, the architect
Nathan Silver, co-author with Charles Jencks
of the influential book of architectural theory
Adhocism (1972).

Dominik Arni, Paulo Zambelli (2009–10)

1652

The Jamaica Wine House

City of London, EC3V 9DS

The complex story of the Jamaica Wine House sheds light on the city's history of internationalism and its bloody colonial links. A 19th century pub with a basement wine bar, it sits in a medieval alleyway off the Square Mile, having opened as a coffee house, London's first, in 1652. The symbolism of early coffee houses often referenced the drink's 'exotic' origins, but in this case the proprietor had travelled as far as the product. Pascal Rosée had entered London as a manservant in 1651 having been born in Smyrna (part of modern Turkey) and the house was known as the Turk's Head as a result. Its connection to Jamaica is a bit more obscure and problematic; popular history tells us the name commemorates the British invasion of Jamaica in 1655 and it is also believed that 19th century merchants with business interests in the Caribbean met here to organise resistance to the abolition of the slave trade.

1665

The Spotted Dog'

Newham, E7 9NP

Fragments of the Spotted Dog date back to the 15th and 16th centuries with an argument that it once formed part of a royal hunting lodge. Once set in extensive countryside boasting its own cricket ground, which in 1888 became the home of Clapton Football Club, a Victorian advertisement described the Dog's location as 'one of the most pleasant parts of Essex'. The expansion of London in the late 19th and 20th centuries challenged this assertion, and the Dog today is a forlorn derelict timber-framed creature in a sea of suburban brick. Since 2012 there has been a concerted effort by local people to bring the old Dog back to life and a planning application to do just that was approved in 2020.

Below: Clapton Football Club return to the Old Spotted Dog Ground, 1943 © London Borough of Newham Heritage Service

1690
The White Swan

Richmond upon Thames, TW1 3DN

The White Swan has dangled its feet in the Thames since the 17th century, located at a particularly good moment on the river's journey where it becomes narrow and bucolic passing by Eel Pie Island. The current building is 18th century with a series of 19th century extensions and terraces built onto the front. High tide times are chalked on the facade and an eminently floodable beer garden directly abuts the river. The White Swan was the original headquarters of the Twickenham Yacht Club from 1897 until a purpose-built clubhouse was commissioned in 1924. With the yachts out of the way, the tradition of an annual 'raft race' could begin in the 1970s. Contestants in fancy dress race their homemade craft across the river to Ham and back again, driven on in part by the beer festival in full swing back at the pub.

1691
The Plume of Feathers

Greenwich, SE10 9LZ

The Queen's House, Inigo Jones' Palladian masterpiece in Greenwich, was originally designed to sit astride the main road heading south-east out of the capital. Anyone leaving the city by this route would, a few moments after the Queen's House, have arrived at the Plume of Feathers, the first Coaching Inn on the road to Kent. This lasted for about nine years, because in 1699 Lord Romney, responsible for the upkeep of Greenwich Park, relocated the highway closer to the river. Queen's House lost its internal road and the Plume lost its passing trade. Yet the pub's backstreet location, facing the park, is now part of what makes it a pleasure. The Rose family have been landlords since 1980 and have run the pub independently since 1999.

1773

Ye Olde Mitre

Camden, EC1N 6SJ

A blue bishop's mitre, fixed to a lamppost,
is the only sign of this pub from the street.
Follow the mitre down a tight alleyway and
you'll find the Mitre, an 18th century building
on the site of a tavern which originally catered
for servants of the Bishop of Ely. The pub
itself is a compact series of extremely dark
and evocative timber-panelled rooms, which
feel ancient but are largely a 20th century
pastiche. Most people spend their time here
in the alley outside the pub, gathering around
barrels and leaning against brick walls.
Drinking in this context feels like inhabiting
the cloisters and courts of the medieval city.
Improbably, a cherry tree embedded in the
Mitre's facade still marks the former boundary
of the Bishop of Ely's land.

Yẹmí Aládérun, Stuart Darling, Alex Jenkins, Rob McCarthy
(2009–10)

The Spaniards

Barnet, NW3 7JJ

The Spaniards played a surprising role in the Gordon Riots of 1780, the largest and bloodiest rioting in London's history to date, during which the term 'King Mob' – forever associated with the power of the proletariat – was first used. One of the rioters' targets was the serving Lord Chief Justice, William Murray, first Earl of Mansfield, who lived at Kenwood House at the northern edge of Hampstead Heath, a few miles from the centre of the city. Like countless others before and since, the rioters stopped at the Spaniards, then a coaching Inn and toll point on the road out of London, to refresh and recuperate. The quick-thinking landlord supplied a large quantity of free beer whilst sending word to the army of the rioters' intentions. As a result the riot never reached Kenwood and King Mob was once again undone by the counter-revolutionary power of alcohol.

The White Raven*

Tower Hamlets, E1 2EG

The Committee for the Relief of the Black Poor was founded in 1786 to tackle the mistreatment of the African and Asian diaspora in London, a cause which overlapped with the abolitionist and anti-slavery movement. At the time, Marylebone and Mile End were home to significant communities of black and Asian Londoners so Inns in both locations were selected as distribution points for money, food, and clothing. These were the Yorkshire Stingo in Marylebone and the White Raven Tavern in Mile End. Neither now exist, but the site of the White Raven has since 1876 been the home of the Whitechapel Mission, a charity dedicated to assisting London's rough sleepers.

539 THE SPANIARDS INN. HAMPSTEAD HEATH.

SERIES OF 18 No 17

ST. GEORGE'S TAVERNS INN SIGNS

AVERAGE CONTENTS 50 MADE IN FINLAND

GRENADIER,

18 Wilton Row,
Belgrave Square,
London. S.W.1.

1818

The Grenadier

Westminster, SW1X 7NR

The Grenadier is hard to find, squeezed
into the back of a long mews street in
Belgravia in the space between two grand
crescents and the former barracks of the
Grenadier Guards. When it first opened
it wasn't even intended for public use,
instead serving as the officers' mess for
the barracks, commemorated in a museum's
worth of Guardsmen-related memorabilia.
When it became a public house in 1818, the
Grenadier still only addressed the trades-
men's entrances of the grand terraces of
Belgravia so became a servants' pub which,
in architecture critic Ian Nairn's words,
has since 'short-circuited to become a local
for rich mews-dwellers'. The pub is six steps
higher than the pavement which we like
to think enabled departing guardsmen to
easily access their horses.

1827

The Anglesea Arms

Kensington and Chelsea, SW7 3QG

The Anglesea was built as part of a wave
of 19th century development over what had
previously been market gardens. For the
first hundred years of its life it was a Tied
House, linked to Henry Meux & Co., based
at the Horse Shoe Brewery which from 1764
to 1921 sat – implausibly – at the junction
of Oxford Street and Tottenham Court Road
on the site of what is now the Dominion
Theatre. By the 1960s the Anglesea had
become a Freehouse and, under enlightened
family landlording, championed real ale.

1848

The Oddfellows Arms

Harrow, HA5 3EN

The Beerhouse Act of 1830, which allowed ordinary citizens to serve beer in their own homes under licence from a local magistrate, led to an explosion of new Beerhouses across the country. The Oddfellows seems to have begun in this way, subsequently growing to occupy its whole terrace and gaining a glass frontage stretching across its facade. Etched windows indicate that it once contained both a public and a private bar, accessed by different doors. All that said, it's still tiny, and has the atmosphere of an unfussy rural pub with clear domestic origins.

1848

The Sutton Arms

Islington, EC1M 6EB

On a street corner one block back from the main road, the Sutton is an archetypal London boozer open since the 19th century, when corner pubs were a ubiquitous part of the development of Victorian London, often providing neat, sociable knuckles to streets of terraced housing. A Freehouse run by Mike Guignan since 1991 and in recent years aided by his son Jack, it stocks an extraordinarily well-chosen and cared-for ramp of beer that is among the best in the city. The quality of the beer – and the quality of the thinking behind it – is all the more remarkable given the brilliantly informal and unselfconscious running of the place, which is highly personal and relaxed. The Sutton is a landmark to the idea that being a 'proper boozer' doesn't mean rejecting the wonderful things happening in contemporary brewing.

c.1850

The Case is Altered

Hillingdon, HA5 2EW

The Case is Altered sits alongside Eastcote cricket ground in a more or less picture-perfect village green scenario, which is remarkable given that it is surrounded by suburbs, carefully hidden in the bushes. Parts of the pub date to the 16th century but it was rebuilt in the 19th and then remodelled again in a consciously (but very successfully) 'olde worlde' manner during the interwar period. The name of the pub is surprisingly common but its actual origin as a phrase is hotly contested, with various stories pointing to Spanish origins (*Casa Alta*) through to legal commentaries on the behaviour of former landlords. We'll almost certainly never know but the speculation is better than discovering the truth.

c.1850

The Three Crowns

Hackney, N1 6AD

A mid-19th century corner pub that has some-how survived the intensive redevelopment around Old Street roundabout, the Three Crowns was renovated in 2013 to reveal an original tiled frontage declaring in embossed glazed lettering 'BARCLAY'S STOUT AND ALES'. Such signage would once have been ubiquitous in London as in the early 19th century Barclay, Perkins & Co owned the world's largest brewery, the Anchor Brewery in Bermondsey. Stout came first at the Anchor because it had been supplying its ten per cent Imperial stout to the Russian state since the 1780s thanks to a treaty with Catherine the Great only ceasing production in 1993.

1859

The Queen's Arms

Kensington and Chelsea, SW7 5QL

Like the Grenadier (p37) a mile or so to the east, this pub on a mews corner would have likely started out catering to the coachmen and servants of the large mid-Victorian terraced houses that backed onto it. The area was built out rapidly in the wake of the 1851 Great Exhibition which took place immediately to the north. Regular patrons of the pub today include students and tutors at Imperial College, the Royal College of Art and the Royal College of Music, all institutions with origins in the enormous cultural project of Albertopolis.

1867
The Trafalgar Tavern

Greenwich, SE10 9NW

Sitting directly on the edge of the Thames at Greenwich, the Trafalgar is unusually lavish for its date, presenting a grand stuccoed facade to the river comprising large bay windows and bowed lead canopies. Its pomp is partly a response to Christopher Wren and Nicholas Hawksmoor's Old Royal Naval College which it sits alongside and partly due to Greenwich's status as a resort in the 18th and 19th centuries, accessed from central London by boat. By the 1860s, the Liberal Party's whitebait dinners at the Trafalgar, following a river journey from the Palace of Westminster, was an annual fixture. Inside the pub is filled with light, pale and Neoclassical. It's really an intricate work of postwar restoration but, thanks to the river, it works.

Trafalgar Tavern, Greenwich, etching by James Tissot, 1878. Courtesy Metropolitan Museum

1865
The Royal Oak

Bexley, DA6 8JS

Mary Ann 'Polly' Elms ran the Royal Oak from 1865 to her death in 1894. In that time, her reputation for keeping the pub spotless – particularly its internal staircase – led to a nickname which remains today: Polly Cleanstairs. To the street, the pub presents a beautifully asymmetrical white weatherboarded elevation. Alongside it sits a black-painted 'crinkly tin' shed, built in the 1920s to provide the pub with a dance hall and locals with a community centre, polling station, bingo hall, function room, club-house for the West Kent Road Cycling Club and a meeting room for the local Woodcraft Folk group. Today the Polly Hall still shares its yard with the pub and is home to a nursery school.

41

1871

The Blue Posts

Westminster, W1T 3ET

Laura C. Forster

The Blue Posts sits at the corner of Newman Street and Eastcastle Street. There has been a pub on this site since 1762, after this part of Fitzrovia was first developed in the 1730s by the land and slave-owner William Berners. By the mid-19th century the district was the incandescent heart of radical and socialist life in London, and its pubs provided much needed sanctuary and sustenance for a motley crowd of continental Communists, revolutionary refugees, and British republicans.

Amid the innumerable pubs of the area, the Blue Posts is particularly notable as it was the preferred meeting place of a number of political refugees who had escaped to London following the defeat of the Paris Commune. As a result, the pub became a place of conviviality and commiseration as exiles struggled through the disappointment of defeat and the heavy burden of homesickness, and forged new connections with their radically-inclined neighbours with whom they shared pints and political proclivities.

The Paris Commune was a radical experiment in government. Following the Franco-Prussian war, Paris democratically elected a 'Commune' council in March 1871 which governed the city for 72 days passing measures such as the abolition of night work, free secular education, the separation of Church and State, and the cancellation of rent arrears accrued by starving Parisians during the Siege of Paris the year before. In May the Commune was brutally defeated during a week of bloodshed, and more than 10,000 Communards were killed. Following this defeat, thousands fled France to avoid imprisonment, deportation, or death.

As a result, and due in large part to Britain's liberal asylum policy at the time, around 3,500 refugees – some 1,500 Communards and their families – arrived in Britain in the 1870s. The largest concentration of these refugees settled in Fitzrovia. Here Communard exiles lodged, worked, socialised, published political addresses and newspapers, and expanded some of the mutual aid networks and organisations established by earlier French communities in London who had been banished by the Second Empire in the mid-century.

The Blue Posts had already been adopted in 1856 as the headquarters of the French mutual assistance association, the *Société des Indépendants*, with its upstairs meeting room thereafter dubbed the *Salle des Indépendants*. A sceptical reporter from the conservative *Standard* described the room as 'a large apartment furnished with rows of tables and the usual appointments of the common room of British hostelries. An engraved portrait of Joseph Hume was almost the first ornament that struck me on entering; that was reassuring. On the wall was a board painted "Club of Independents, founded 1856, enrolled 1858"! From 1871 the *Salle des Indépendants* became a key gathering place for exiled Communards. The room was used regularly by their largest and most comprehensive Communard society, *La Société des Réfugiés de la Commune à Londres*, which offered practical relief, comradery, and political solidarity to all those who had fought for the Commune. Leeds-born Communard Adolphe Smith, who ran free English classes for political exiles in Francis Street (now Torrington Place), just off Tottenham Court Road, remembered that 'at the Blue Posts... foreign refugees of all nationalities, and their inevitable suite of foreign police spies, indulge in continental drinks, and enjoy a few moments of leisure and chat'.

Smith attended several meetings of the Communard section of the *Société des Indépendants*, often referred to as the Red Benevolent Society. At a meeting in September 1871, with more than 70 attendees present (including a handful of women Commune militants) in the crowded *Salle* – 'all peaceably sitting at the tables smoking cigarettes or long clay pipes, taking pulls out of tankards of beer, or eating bread and

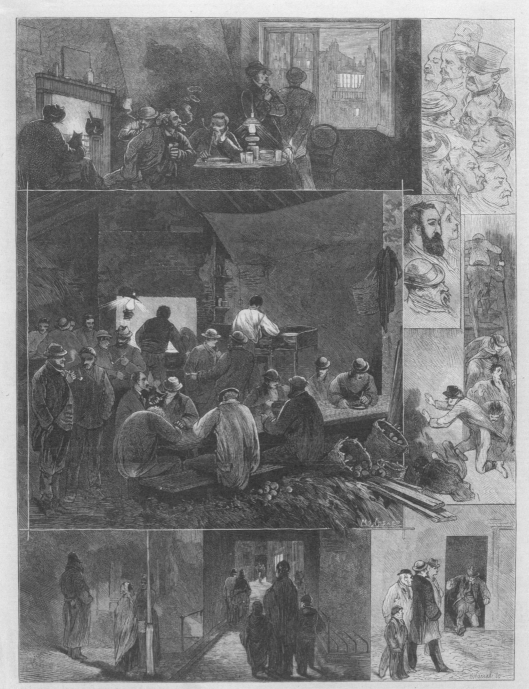

THE COMMUNIST REFUGEES' CO-OPERATIVE KITCHEN IN NEWMAN PASSAGE

cheese' – Smith noted that 'every effort is made to collect money or offers of work and these are distributed according to the requirements of each member'. This was mutual aid; the voluntary reciprocal exchange of resources and services organised by a community set on keeping each other afloat by whatever means they could muster. For exiled Communards, mutual aid was a political project – organising in the pub was a way of enacting a politics that insisted on co-operation rather than competition as its fundamental principle. 'The constitution of the society is ideally democratic', Adolphe Smith explained, 'a committee of nine is elected by means of the *scrutin de liste* [proportional representation] and absolute majority. At the end of every month lots are drawn, and the three members they designate are obliged to withdraw. An election refills these posts and thus an infusion of now blood is constantly secured, and the society is guaranteed from the government of a clique'.

Some of the contributions extracted at the Blue Posts were used to fund a co-operative soup kitchen for struggling refugee Communards. *La Marmite* was established across the road and slightly north of the Blue Posts, in Newman Passage. It was 'situated on the top floor of so wretched a building that there was not space for a staircase'. Instead, Smith recalls, it was reached by 'means of a ladder with a very greasy rope that served in the stead of a balustrade. But here any refugee who could prove that he had fought for the Paris Commune was able to obtain a meal for twopence'.

The activities of exiled Communards in Fitzrovia, and their modes of political organisation, were not incongruous with the area. Fitzrovia had long been established as a dissident neighbourhood, and strident politics had long animated the pub chat here. In the second half of the 19th century a host of activists – mostly secularists, freethinkers, old Chartists, O'Brienites, and members of the Land and Labour League and other radical clubs – operated their outfits out of the pubs, meeting rooms and halls of Fitzrovia. The *Hotel de la Boule d'Or* on Percy Street was the reputed birthplace of the International Working Mens' Association (IWMA) in 1864, and in the early 1870s the association met regularly in nearby Rathbone Street. Following the events of the Commune the police were so concerned with the activities of the IWMA that they threatened to withdraw the licences from any victuallers who allowed branches to meet in their pub rooms.

This club culture was a salient feature of metropolitan politics in Victorian London. Clubs were mutual improvement societies, where political and intellectual opinions were formed and organised. The pub had long offered working people the facilities for social, political and economic intercourse, and club life helped to formalise some of these connections. In some cases, the club might have its own premises or rent a regular room, but more often, the club premises *was* the pub. Working class artisans would listen, lecture, debate, and argue, often accompanied by a beer and, afterwards, a game of billiards. Contributors were expected to be reasoned and intellectually engaged, but strangers and fledgling speakers were encouraged. James Macdonald of the Social Democratic Federation (the first explicitly Socialist organisation in Britain) remembered discovering Socialism in Fitzrovia in precisely this manner in 1881: 'it was at a public-house near Tottenham Street that I first made the acquaintance of some of the London Socialists', wrote Macdonald.

'There was a Scottish Club held there, of which I was a member, and one evening the landlord told us that there was a meeting being held in another room of some of the most red-hot Fenians and dynamiters in England. Some of us were curious to see these fellows'. This curiosity led Macdonald into the other room, and the Socialists he met there irrevocably altered the course of his political development.

Encounters of this kind were commonplace in 19th century Fitzrovia; persons might arrive in the pub for one meeting and end up joining another. Or one might arrive solely with the intention of having a quiet drink, and wind up embroiled in a heated debate about the possible merits of direct democracy. In other words, the serendipity of the pub facilitated the introduction of new political, social and intellectual pursuits and commitments.

Soon the German *émigré* Communist Club also made the upstairs of the Blue Posts their home in the mid-1870s, and members would have crossed paths with Communards and others in the bar area. This politicised socialisation helped to create links between British, French, and international activists, and mirrored some of the associational cultures that had been so important under the Commune itself. As one *London Echo* journalist put it, revolutionary refugees in London created 'a veritable realisation of their pet and primary idea – *Fraternité*'.

For the political refugees of the Paris Commune and their internationalist neighbours in Fitzrovia, the Blue Posts was an informal political forum, a cosmopolitan debating society, a mutual aid association; it was a job centre, a library, and a reading room. In a world of short-lived political organisations and shifting political fragments, pubs are the archives of the informal conversations, the heated debates, the intimate gatherings, and the impromptu meetings that were as important to the development of Socialist ideas in Britain as the official political programmes and ideological tracts of the period.

The Blue Posts exemplifies the associational culture that was at the heart of many expansive political projects in the 19th century. The pub was not just the setting for political discussion – it was politics in action. This pub politics wasn't just idle talk – the public house was a place to enact radical visions for the future: it was civic life in microcosm.

Previous: The Communist Refugees Co-operative Kitchen in Newman Passage, *The Graphic* February 3 1872.
© Museum of London

1880
The Tabard

Hounslow, W4 1LW

Bedford Park is a suburb conceived in the 1870s by developer Jonathan Carr and advertised at the time as 'the healthiest place in the world'. Its leafy streets, red-brick detached villas and public spaces defined by hedges were globally influential. Unlike later garden cities and suburbs such as at Letchworth and Welwyn, Carr's 'Arts and Crafts principles' were mostly aesthetic, which meant that pubs were allowed. Richard Norman Shaw, one of the most admired architects of the day and a man of multiple modes and styles, had designed house types for Bedford Park, and his design for the Tabard is folky, jovial and medievalist. It includes tiling by potter, novelist and close friend of William Morris, William de Morgan, depicting nursery scenes – an unusual theme for a public house. In the spirit of Inns long gone, the Tabard hosts a 96-seater theatre upstairs.

Below: Joy Mulandi

1893
The Royal Oak

Brent, NW10 4TS

The Royal Oak was built at the peak of confidence in the multi-roomed, palatial town centre pub. It commands a high street corner of Harlesden and is the final flourish of a long terrace of baroque-ish red brick and stucco commercial buildings. The pub has been gutted and refurbished several times and is clearly a lot plainer inside than it once was, but an extraordinary tiled wall depicting King Charles hiding up a tree (the original Royal Oak) survives in what now serves as a fire escape.

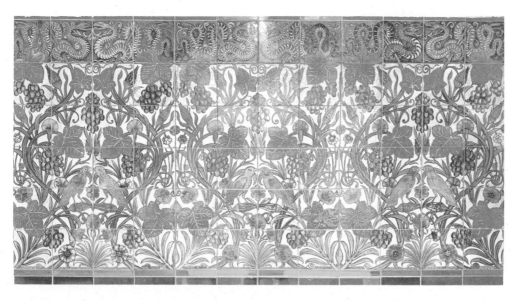

1896

The King's Head

Wandsworth, SW17 7PB

Music halls – sentimental, populist and brash – emerged out of the saloon bars of urban pubs in the middle of the 19th century and the two often shared space until the London County Council banned drinking in performance spaces in 1914. William Mortimer Brutton was a prolific designer of pubs, music halls, and pub-cum-music halls and the Kings Head in Tooting is perhaps his masterpiece. It was described very precisely by Mark Girouard as a 'mini palace for a fat boozy king'; a facade of balconies, false windows, baroque scrolls, literal king's heads, urns and even the face of the landlord sculpted into a bracket, all inside a large single room divided by expressive glass screens. The whole thing is rakish and self-confident – High Victorian popular taste given civic expression.

1896

The Swan and Sugar Loaf

Croydon, CR2 6EA

The current building, elaborate and picturesque with an Arts and Crafts roofline, was the terminus of the Croydon tramway and something of a travellers' pub on the Brighton Road heading south out of town. Its peculiar name is most likely a combination of the Swan – a fairly typical name for a coaching Inn – and an adjacent bakery sited to appeal to travellers. Built by Overton's, who brewed in Surrey Street in the heart of Croydon, it is an extremely confident and gregarious building that defines the suburban high street in which it sits. Today, unfortunately and in an increasingly common condition, the pub's impact on the locality has outlasted its life as a public house. A Tesco Express since 2012, the building stands relatively unscathed externally and its decorative signage has been retained. The pub continues to give its name to the area and to the adjacent bus garage, a legacy of the tramway system, and even beyond the grave tells stories of Croydon's history and growth.

1898

The Star and Garter

Bromley, BR1 1NZ

An almost psychedelic reimagining by
architects Berner & Son of commercial
vernacular architecture, dating from the
short period of incredibly exuberant public
house design when ancient Inns across
the city were being torn down and replaced
by complex, multi-layered 'hotels' offering
a bewildering series of forms and spaces.
In this case the Star's protruding turret,
voluptuous plasterwork and Mock-Tudor
half-timbering (that doesn't even try to look
structural) would not be out of place in a
fantasy novel. Not many pubs of this type
were this well-made or well crafted — for
example the extraordinarily accomplished
mosaic at the threshold (detail overleaf).

1898

The Viaduct Tavern

City of London, EC1A 7AA

Gin Palaces defined themselves in opposition
to the ordinariness, austerity and homeliness
of the Beerhouse. They did so by leaning hard
toward glamour, femininity, complexity and
richness. The first purpose-built examples
materialised in London in the late 1820s.
But it was the end of the century before the
architecture caught up and became the
defining image of the urban pub; cut glass,
elaborate timberwork, bespoke ceramics,
all of which combined to make a fantastical
environment which is urban and bustling but
also cut off from the street – otherworldly.
The Viaduct was built in 1865 in a tough,
flattened Neoclassical style, and was named
after the nearby Holborn Viaduct, newly
completed by city surveyor William Haywood.
But a renovation by Arthur Dixon, beginning
in 1898, gave it the archetypal Gin Palace
interior that we see today. Though commercially adventurous, the wistful floor-to-ceiling
pre-Raphaelite paintings hint at a more
backward looking future.

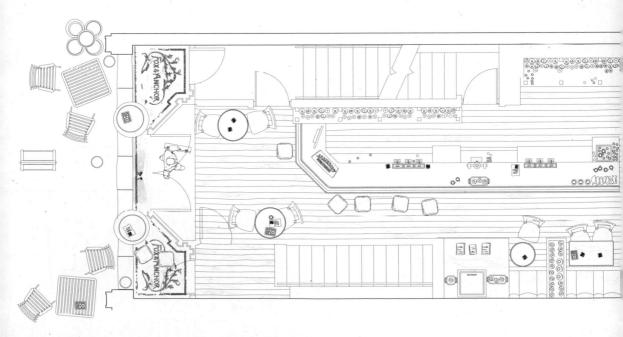

1898

The Fox and Anchor

Islington, EC1M 6AA

One street back from Smithfield meat market, the Fox and Anchor's bar opens at 7am to cater for weary butchers clocking off all-night shifts though author of *London Pubs*, Alan Reeve-Jones, fresh from an all-night party, found it hard to get served in full dinner dress in 1962. One of London's few remaining Early Houses, its front elevation by Latham Augustus Withall is entirely ceramic and has been described as 'English Art Nouveau' – which here means that the sensual curves of proper Art Nouveau co-exist with the geometries of a medieval townhouse. The interior is partially original but also the work of several eras of renovation and refurbishment. The highlight is a series of private booths, set deep into the pub's plan, from which it is hard to tear yourself away.

Timothy Hare, Tobin McCloy, Christopher Taylor, Rachel Vallance (2009–10)

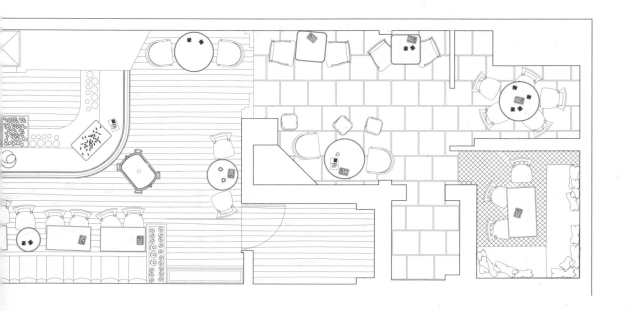

1899

The Salisbury

Haringey, N4 1JX

John Cathles Hill was an architect and developer responsible for building, in the late 19th century, most of the middle-class suburb of Harringay, comprising some 2000 houses plus high streets. When his supply chain of bricks started to run dry he bought a brickworks in Fletton, Cambridgeshire and in doing so built the world's largest brick kiln, popularising the Fletton brick that can now be seen everywhere in the city. Each of Hill's suburbs was gifted with a palatial public house on a prominent corner, and the Salisbury is the grandest of them. When it opened in Summer 1899 it was deemed 'one of the finest hotels to exist' by the trade press of its day. Among London's greatest pub interiors, the Salisbury includes a former billiard room at the rear crowned with a large glazed skylight decorated as if thronged with vines.

Above: Bar interior © London Metropolitan Archives / LCC Photograph Library

1901
The Castle Inn

Harrow, HA1 3EF

Low-key, elegantly proportioned and well-sited halfway up Harrow-on-the-Hill, the Castle is a roughcast and colourwashed 1901 pub notable for its elegant, understated exterior and well-preserved interior. A rear billiard room (now used as a dining room) retains pretty wooden 'linenfold' panelling imitating hanging fabric. The Castle exemplifies the quieter end of late-Victorian pub architecture, as if Charles Voysey had a quiet word with Norman Shaw to calm him down a bit.

1904
The Fox

Enfield, N13 4JD

Before London Transport was established in 1933, public transport in London was delivered by a multitude of different businesses including public houses. Belinda and Robert Davey, licensees of the 1870s Fox, ran a horse-drawn bus into central London from the pub for many years and are credited with inventing the spiral stair method of accessing a bus' upper storey. As a result of their bus operation, when rebuilt in 1904 the pub boasted a large rear yard with stables, coach house, tea garden and skittles alley. At the time of writing, that yard is being redeveloped into around 50 apartments and the pub is also under refurbishment as part of the works.

Below: The Davey family © Enfield Local Studies and Archive

1904

The Boleyn

Newham, E6 1PW

The Boleyn was built in 1900 in a florid
Gin Palace aesthetic with a billiard hall
to rival the Salisbury (p54) in Harringay.
But, four years later, West Ham United
turned up and began renting the adjacent
Boleyn Ground as their home pitch (which
it remained until the club relocated to the
Queen Elizabeth Olympic Park's London
Stadium in 2016) making the Boleyn a
real 'supporters pub', often boarded on
match days and boasting an extraordinary
collection of club-related artefacts. At the
time of writing, the Boleyn is being
refurbished to an exacting standard while
an unlovely new bar within the London
Stadium is named the Boleyn in tribute.

1905

The Blackfriar

City of London, EC4V 4DY

Probably the world's first theme pub, or
at least the moment when pub architecture
becomes mannerist and self-referential,
not only channelling past styles and historical conditions but creating fictional ones.
A free, loose art nouveau is used inside and
out to make a place which reimagines the
black-robed monks of the Dominician friary
that used to exist on the site as free-living
revellers full of worldly advice written on the
walls in elaborate, beautifully crafted tiling
and carving. In contrast to Gin Palaces, the
Blackfriar is deeply personal and obsessive,
and also extremely homely with most of the
pub feeling like a large inglenook fireplace.
It is the work of individual craftspeople and
visionaries, among them idiosyncratic
architect Harold Herbert Fuller-Clark,
rather than of industrialisation and brewery-
approved common sense.

Above and right: © Architectural Press Archive /
RIBA Collections

The Trafalgar Freehouse

Merton, SW19 2JY

A humble corner Freehouse with a strong character, the 'Traf' dates from the middle of the 19th century, when it was a pure Alehouse only licensed to sell ale and cider. It was enlarged and renovated in around 1910 and its character is very much of that period – austere, homely – all the ingredients of an Improved Pub but squeezed onto a tiny street corner. The pub hosts blues and New Orleans-style jazz, puts a lot of thought into its beer selection, has its own cricket team, and once a year hosts the Greensleeves Morris Men who perform their mummers' play in the bar.

The Brewery Tap

Hounslow, TW8 8BD

The Brewery Tap is a great city contrast, a delicate Arts and Crafts-influenced detached pub stranded in a sea of picturesque industrial estate between Brentford High Street and the Grand Union Canal just as it reaches the Thames. This isolated position is entirely to its benefit as it puts on live music a minimum of four nights a week and can turn the volume up to 11! The pub was once part of the Grand Junction Brewery, later bought by Fuller's and rebuilt around 1908.

1913
The Lord Clyde
Southwark, SE1 1ER

The Clyde is a transitional pub, between the opulence of high Victorian and the austerity of the early 20th century. It was built by Truman, Hanbury, Buxton & Co., which at the time was one of the world's largest brewers, running huge breweries at Spitalfields and Burton upon Trent. Like many other industrial-scale brewers, Truman's were trying to develop an identifiable house-style for their pubs and to boost their appeal to wider audiences. The Clyde was an early attempt, with distinctive green faience celebrating the name and iconography of the brewer. It may be an early work of Arthur Sewell, who designed over 50 pubs between 1910 and 1940, many of which were for Truman's. The pub's interior is an unfussy survivor, thanks to being run by three generations of the same family between 1956 and 2020.

Below: Ewan Munro

1914
King Edward VII
Newham, E15 4BQ

The names of pubs sometimes define a whole area; the Elephant and Castle, the Nags Head. Others are a bit more changeable. The King of Prussia was built in the early 18th century but with the outbreak of the first world war swiftly changed its name to the more patriotic King Edward VII. Probably the lowest building in Stratford, beyond its pedimented doors lies a warren of different bars, and an attractive Victorian tiled and glazed wall in the entrance passageway.

1915

The Cock*

Sutton, SM1 1DJ

The Cock was an ancient Inn at the centre
of Sutton that was demolished in 1898 in
order to widen the main road, but its sign
was such a landmark that it outlived the pub
and remains in place today. In 1915 sign posts
to nearby towns were added, and a hundred
years later the sign was Grade-II listed.

The Mothers Arms

Tower Hamlets, E3 5SB

Clare Cumberlidge
Ruth Ewan

Clare Cumberlidge My work engages with the public and the public realm, collaborating with artists to enrich and support the complexity of public space and encounters. I am interested in the active relationship between art and everyday life, making the pub an ideal site of enquiry. I wanted to talk with you because the public house recurs in your work. Your art practice deals with the circulation of radical ideas and forms of social organisation, and you have used the pub in different ways – as a site for the production of and engagement with culture, and as a source of language. If you could take us to any London pub today, which would it be?

Ruth Ewan To the Mothers Arms, which once stood on Old Ford Road, Bow, opposite Gunmakers Wharf that housed the London Small Arms Factory, an important arms producer during the first world war. In 1915 the activist, artist and suffragette Sylvia Pankhurst took over no. 438, an ex-public house called the Gunmakers Arms, and as a pacifist, she renamed it the Mothers Arms. This was one of many buildings taken over by the East London Federation of Suffragettes (ELFS) around this time.

Some 40 children were cared for in the facility, run by Lucy Burgis and Minnie Lansbury. It was a clinic for mothers and babies, a creche allowing mothers to work, and provided information on hygiene and nutrition. Maud Hebbes, a nurse at the Mothers Arms, was later the first nurse at the birth control clinic of Marie Stopes. The nursery followed the radical Montessori educational method, using child-sized furniture that allowed them to take part in self-directed learning and play. The main bar area became the reception from which medicines and fresh eggs were distributed. The parlour became a doctor's surgery and upstairs was the nursery. Later, they opened a soup kitchen to feed the local poor.

When we think about the history of pubs we might think of a typically male, working class culture surrounding them. But if we go back to pre-industrialisation when brewing was a decentralised process, it actually took place on a domestic scale and was carried out by women called 'alewives'. Gradually within communities people would go to alewives' houses to drink and then to buy ale. It was tradition that when the ale had brewed the alewife would place an ale stake outside the house – transforming the home into a public space and, in turn, establishing the traditional pub sign hanging on a pole. I love how Pankhurst keeps that tradition of the pub name but reclaims the pub as a female space.

CC So the public house began as a house or a home, under the control of a woman with a means of independence. That balance and switch between public and private is fascinating and speaks to the often-overlooked radical history and potential of the domestic space. Why does the Mothers Arms resonate with you in our moment?

RE It reveals so much about this period in history, the on-the-ground relief work the ELFS were doing, of women supporting women, but also I love the poetics of it. I see it as an early act of *détournement* [the tactic of hijacking mainstream cultural infrastructure]. By altering the pub name she creates a powerful gesture of feminist subversion. Sylvia was an artist before she was an activist – she said she gave up art because she saw starvation and need within her community. It has a lot in common with much of the mutual aid work we see going on now. It also shows how intersectional

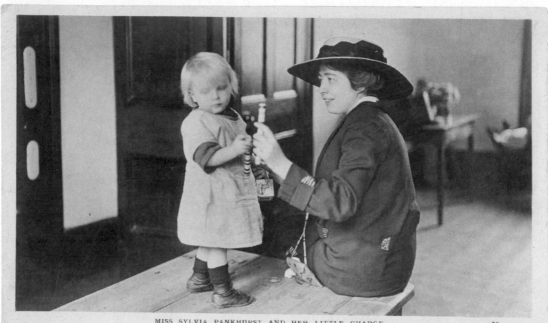

MISS SYLVIA PANKHURST AND HER LITTLE CHARGE
THE EAST LONDON FEDERATION OF SUFFRAGETTES

Sylvia Pankhurst (1882–1960)
playing with a child in the
Mother's Arms, 1913–16.
© Museum of London

her activism was – she wasn't just out to win women the vote.

I first learned about the Mothers Arms through a residency with Chisenhale Gallery in 2009–2010. I wanted to make work with a series of secondary schools on the radical micro-history within reach of the school playgrounds. The feminist history project came out of the school at St Paul's Way with a group of year eight and nine boys. I remember asking in the first session what history was and one of the boys said 'History is war, Miss!'.

By the end, the boys had visited the Women's Library and we had walked all around Mile End and Bow to trace sites of radical historic significance. Sheila Rowbotham, the feminist historian, and I led a public walking tour around the area. I think working on that project changed my own relationship with East London, in fact every city since. We can think about the city as a classroom of sorts, as a series of peda-gogical object lessons.

CC The pub itself can be seen as a sort of urban classroom or cultural incubator – cultures handed down, produced, main-tained and shared in the intimate social and communal space of the pub. We can all think of particular pubs that hold the history, values and cultures of communities.

RE I find pubs fascinating spaces. I don't mean bars and shiny new places, but proper old established pubs and the unique ecosystems within. But I do have a love-hate relationship with pub culture. As a woman, growing up in a small town in Fife there were certain pubs you'd just know not to go in – if you looked a bit different, or were gay, then pubs could be dangerous places. It's the same now living in Glasgow – there are pubs I would not dream of going into as a woman. The pubs designed with fights in mind – no windows and screwed down tables; the sectarian pubs.

There is a song by Scottish musician Aidan Moffat called *Where You Are Meant to Be*, a funny story about going around a few different pubs with friends and ending up in places you find scary or too posh, then finally ending up in the right place – it really sums up my feeling about a good pub:

> And so that's now where we are
> We're standing swaying by the bar
> Catching eyes full of grog and glee
> Jimmy gets a round and pays
> Raises a pint and proudly says
> 'You always come to where you're
> meant to be'

CC Ownership and control are also signifi-cant – I am thinking here of the kind of semi-public clubs such as Working Men's Clubs and Fishermen's Clubs as well as more recent community-owned pubs. In 2008 I co-published *Society*, a book by artist Bridget Smith documenting the interiors of London's clubs and associations – a record of the social infrastructure and lived culture of the city through self-organised spaces including the Turkish Community Centre, the General Brown Moth Club, the Spiritualist Association, the Vintners' Hall. These clubs asserted an identity and also suggested a form of alternative economy, staffed and maintained by volunteers and communities. I know you have been looking at examples of radical models of organisation of pubs.

RE Recently I've been researching a net-work of pubs called The Gothenburg System which grew out of the mining communities in Fife and East Lothian. It was, and still is,

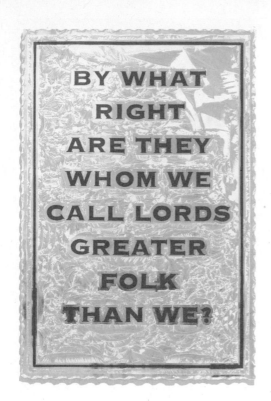

BY WHAT
RIGHT
ARE THEY
WHOM WE
CALL LORDS
GREATER
FOLK
THAN WE?

Above: Mirrors for Princes
(John Ball), Ruth Ewan 2019

Opposite: A Feminist Jukebox
of People Trying to Change the
World, Ruth Ewan 2018

Overleaf: Feminist Beer Mat
no 1 (Mary Wollstonecraft),
Ruth Ewan 2019

a really inspiring model, what we would now perhaps call a social enterprise where 95% of the pubs' profits go back into local projects. In Fife the Goths, as they were known, funded some of the first community midwives and ambulances. In Newtongrange, the Dean Tavern still operates on a similar model. In recent years profits have supported local groups including the Newtongrange Silver Band, the Newbattle Beekeepers Association, Newtongrange Star Football Club and the Newtongrange Children's Gala.

CC When we consider how much time artists spend in pubs there are surprisingly few paintings of the interiors of pubs. The pub recurs in your work, not just as a subject, but also as a place to produce work and as a source of language or form. For example, you have made pub mirrors and beer mats and jukeboxes.

RE Where I'm from, people are very sceptical of contemporary art and I think this was a way to make something familiar and non-intimidating. The first work for a pub was a lamp carved out of turnips that I made with a friend at art school. We wired it up and it was beautiful as the light shone through the thin slices of vegetable. It was a bit of a joke, as in Scotland you never used to get pumpkins so at Halloween we used to carve neep lanterns.

In 2003 I started working on *A Jukebox of People Trying to Change the World* and that really has been a labour of love. Most jukeboxes are centrally controlled through subscription services now but I really like the 'homebrew' ones you don't get much of these days where owners in pubs were making compilation CDs with their own labels.

The beer mats came more recently, partially in response to the Wetherspoons

pro-Brexit beer mats. The first one was for an event with the Whitechapel Gallery where they showed the feminist version of the jukebox in a local pub. I remember seeing an image of a protest against one of those Jack the Ripper walking tours. I can't stand that culture of violence as entertainment around those tours so I wanted to make a feminist beer mat, quoting Mary Wollstonecraft – it says 'VIRTUE CAN ONLY FLOURISH AMONG EQUALS'. I like the idea that people can take them home or that maybe they will get beer spilled on them. They will naturally disperse.

CC There have been a few galleries occupying the upper floors of pubs where the art inhabited what would have been the function room – the Queen's Elm in Fulham in the 1970s, the Approach Gallery in the 1990s. Traditional art spaces typically come freighted with meaning and the form of space through which people approach and encounter art impacts on the nature of that encounter. The public house combines the implied open access of a public space with the domesticity and scale of the home. Does this create something special in the way people experience art in a pub?

RE Yes I think so. Because many people are less intimidated – they are less hostile towards the object, or the idea, more open. As part of *Sympathetic Magick* for the Edinburgh Art Festival in 2018 I worked with magicians to create a series of political magic tricks. Some were performed in pubs and some up-close, one-to-one at pub tables. We repeated the performances in different types of spaces around Edinburgh and by far the most special encounter was at Sandy Bells, a famous folk music pub. The magician Billy Reid and I devised a 'storydeck

routine' which is when the whole deck of cards is used to tell a visual story. We set it to Dick Gaughan's rendition of Ed Pickford's *Workers Song*. A couple of older guys, regulars, came and watched, they seemed a bit suspicious at first but then they were mesmerised and a couple of them cried. It's to do with the song really, but the magic and the visuals and text added to it. As an artist you don't often get to see on a personal level how people respond to your work, but this was really very important to me.

CC These specific conditions of the pub – familiarity, proximity, intimacy and, of course, alcohol, all provide an environment in which progressive ideas can be expressed, fostered and dispersed, something which seems critical to a healthy sense of public-ness. Sylvia Pankhurst's expanded notion of the Mothers Arms as a centre to nurture and liberate through food, health and education is a continuation of that feminist truth that VIRTUE CAN ONLY FLOURISH AMONG EQUALS, and offers a useful model for a public house of today.

VIRTUE CAN ONLY FLOURISH AMONG EQUALS

1919

The Fitzroy Tavern

Camden, W1T 2LY

In 1919 Judah Kleinfeld, a skilled tailor who had emigrated to Britain from Poland in the 1880s, persuaded the owners of the Hundred Marks pub on Charlotte Street that he and his 15 year-old daughter Annie should be its next tenants. The pub was renamed the Fitzroy Tavern and quickly became one of the most celebrated of its time, partly by creating an atmosphere that attracted some of the era's finest and lushest artists and writers, (among them Nina Hamnett, Dylan Thomas and Augustus John) and partly by running its unique 'Pennies from Heaven' fundraising programme that enabled annual coach trips to the Epsom races and special theatre shows for local children. One year, Charlie Allchild, the driver of the Epsom coach, caught Annie's eye and ended up co-running the Fitzroy into the 1950s. Most of the rest of the story can be had from their daughter Sally Fiber's 1995 'autobiography' of the Tavern, though it was published too early to include a later chapter in the Fitzroy's trajectory: throughout the 1990s and 2000s the pub became a monthly meeting place for *Doctor Who* fans, including figures like Russell T. Davies and Steven Moffat who would later revive the series.

Above: Matt Brown, Overleaf: Throwing 'pennies' at the ceiling at the Fitzroy © Picture Kitchen / Alamy Stock Photo

1920

Cittie of Yorke

Camden, WC1V 6BS

While some interwar pubs went down the road of Neo-Georgian politeness, many others went further back to create a style known, with some disdain, as 'Brewer's Tudor'. *The Architectural Review* in 1947 dismissed the style as a debased caricature, fake and unscholarly. But they were probably trying not to think of the Cittie of Yorke, which is an incredibly (and uniquely) robust and atmospheric example of the style. The main bar is three storeys high with large wine vats looming overhead. Natural light drifts in absentmindedly from high clerestory windows and the edges of the room are divided up into intimate seating booths. It feels urban, by which we mean it feels like a street or courtyard – complex, rich, multi-layered, noisy. Dylan Thomas composed a drinking song at the bar in 1951 which didn't come to light until 2014.

Emilija Blinstrubyte, Aiva Dunauskaite, Maria Ghislanzoni, Neal Kazma, Christopher Kelly (2012)

1922

The Duke's Head

Wandsworth, SW15 1JN

There was a pub here before the annual Oxford and Cambridge boat race, but by the time the current Duke's Head was extensively rebuilt in the 1860s the river and rowing were central to its culture. In 1922 the newly-formed Putney Town Rowing Club adopted the Duke's Head as its home, including a club room on the first floor addressing the river and a cellar with doors directly facing the river for the storage of boats and sculls. The club and the pub were intertwined until 1986.

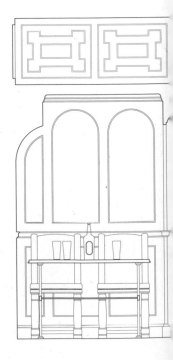

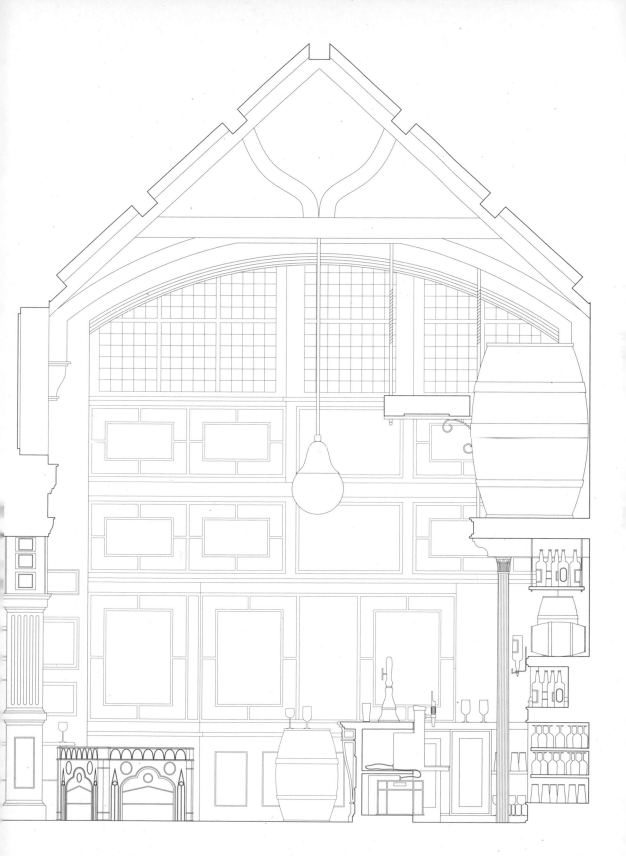

1924

The Fellowship

Lewisham, SE6 3BT

Jessica Boak
Ray Bailey

The Fellowship Inn in Bellingham, South London is historically and culturally significant for several reasons. Firstly, it was the first pub to be built on a local authority housing estate. Secondly, its initial grandeur and subsequent decline are typical of pubs built in this period – so few of which are still around to tell the tale. And finally, it's a promising example of how a monumental suburban pub which was headed for closure can be resuscitated and once again serve its community.

When the London County Council (LCC) started building housing estates to replace slum districts before the first world war, the utopian instinct to create better housing in cleaner neighbourhoods was bundled up with the anti-alcohol Temperance movement. As a result, pubs were a pointed omission. They were a symbol of urban decay – dirty, violent, focal points for crime and prostitution. When the Old Nichol rookery in the East End was demolished in 1890, 12 pubs went with it; the state-of-the-art Boundary Estate which replaced it had none. Nor did the Totterdown Fields Estate (1901), Millbank (1902) or Old Oak in Hammersmith (1905). This replicated a trend in other cities such as Birmingham and Liverpool where

The early 20th century government nationalised and redesigned pubs in Enfield, Cromarty Firth and Carlisle hoping sobriety in signage and architecture (as imposed here on Carlisle's Golden Lion) would temper heavy boozing within. © Cumbria Image Bank (Carlisle Library)

garden villages for workers featured every amenity except somewhere to get a glass of mild ale. And during the first world war Temperance was more or less government policy, with reduced opening hours, beer weakened by legal mandate and even state control of hundreds of pubs. The brewers didn't like where this seemed to be heading, of course, and looked anxiously towards America where prohibition was introduced from 1918. They blustered and lobbied, on the one hand, while on the other adopting a softly-softly approach: what if they came up with their own vision of the ideal pub? A compromise to which local authorities could only say 'Yes'?

The architects of the Improved Public House movement, an alliance of social reformers and progressive brewing industry figures, looked at the Beerhouses and Gin Palaces of the old slum districts and addressed the objections of Temperance campaigners one by one. Improved pubs served food, tea and coffee to discourage non-stop boozing. They weren't gaudy or enticing but, rather, plain to the point of austerity. They were big, bright and airy, deliberately designed without the kind of dark corners and cubby holes where

immoral behaviour might easily play out. Drinkers were encouraged to sit, not to stand at the bar, and there were no spittoons. If this sounds rather muted or even joyless, the brewers reckoned it was better than nothing and at least gave pubs a fighting chance of survival.

The plan worked. In 1922, the London brewer Barclay, Perkins & Co. applied for a licence for a pub to be built on the brand-new Bellingham Estate in South London. They promised a refreshment room, a dining and recreation hall, a roof garden and enough seating to make it possible to do away with bar service all together. It was to be designed by the brewery's in-house architect, F. G. Newnham, in respectable Mock-Tudor style. The Housing of the Working Classes Committee was impressed. After some deliberation, it decided, at last, to abolish the no-pubs policy for LCC estates and the licence was granted.

The Fellowship opened in 1924 as an exemplar for what the pub could be. At the opening ceremony, Admiral Sir Guy Gaunt MP said, 'the days of kissing the barmaid in the back parlour had gone forever' – though whether he regarded this as good or bad news is unclear. The moral purity of this particular pub was further underlined at Christmas 1925 when the vicar and choir of the local church performed a carol concert in the refreshment room, something that would have been unthinkable 30 years earlier. In practice, it was neither dour nor dull. 'It's a regular ragtime show,' one drinker told social commentator Ernest Selley when he visited while researching his 1927 book *The English Public House As It Is*. 'The house gets uncomfortably full on Fridays and Saturdays,' Selley reports, 'and the concerts and dances are very popular with young people.' It gained another floor in 1926 and a children's room in 1927. By 1929, the brewery estimated it was serving more than one million customers per year.

The success of The Fellowship, both commercially and as a social experiment, led Barclay, Perkins & Co. to repeat the approach with pubs such as the famously enormous Downham Tavern. Other breweries joined in too until London, like other cities, had numerous large, handsome pubs serving new estates and suburbs. The architecture was overwhelmingly conservative, designed to recall country houses or an ideal of the village Inn. Inside, pubs were split into a number of different areas, with varying degrees of respectability, usually serviced from a single central bar. Some had ballrooms; others had bowling greens. Most were built with large 'drawing-up spaces' outside to cater for charabanc (an early form of bus) tours, weekend drivers and recreational cyclists. Unfortunately, there was a fundamental problem with the Improved Pub, just as with any other utopian project: it required care and ongoing investment. It also fell out of fashion almost as quickly as it emerged. George Orwell, in *The Road to Wigan Pier* (1937), condemned 'dismal sham Tudor places'; while one of the

main advocates for the Improved Pub, Sydney Nevile of Whitbread, later conceded that 'the public is usually better served by several pubs of moderate size rather than the single super house.' Over the years, the Fellowship, too, lost its sheen. By the 1960s, it was best known for its connection with the boxer Henry Cooper, a Bellingham boy, who occasionally trained on a temporary ring erected in the dance hall. Bands associated with the British blues music boom of the 1960s also played there until, in the 1970s, the function rooms were converted into a disco which ended up attracting aggro and drug dealing – a common story for large interwar suburban pubs.

When we first visited the Fellowship in 2016, it was all but a ruin. Most of the rooms were redundant and shuttered, the pub's limited trade being carried out from the small public bar at the front. With dusty maroon carpets, greasy banquettes, scuffed tables and sickly yellow light, it felt like a timeslip to 1988. The posters insisting 'THIS IS A DRUG FREE PUB' suggested wishful thinking. Behind the scenes, however, the devastation was almost picturesque. Gloomy ground floor rooms untouched in years had an eerie, haunted house quality. Upstairs, the former living quarters and guest rooms were bare, with broken windows, damp wallpaper and shredded lace curtains. The function rooms had dulled discotheque signs, a half-finished game of pool, a forlorn upright piano and ranks of mouldy cinema seating. A South London Marie Celeste.

However, this was not the end of the Fellowship but a turning point. Its gradual abandonment had meant that large parts of the original interior were still intact. We were there as the guests of a housing association, Phoenix, which had bought the pub as part of an overall estate regeneration plan.

Demolition was on the cards, but intervention by Historic England and the London Borough of Lewisham had seen the building listed and registered as an Asset of Community Value, a planning designation which gives local communities the chance to buy a pub before it goes to open market. Phoenix, to its credit, took this on the nose and set about working out how to do something with the building within those limits. There was talk of an on-site brewery, a new cinema, a music rehearsal space, a cafe and more. Would these grand ideas come off?

When we called again a few years later, we found something amazing: the plans, for the most part, had indeed come to fruition. Under a subtly new name, the Fellowship and Star, the pub had reopened – not just one corner of the bar, either, but the entire ground floor. The original wood panelling was stripped and cleaned, complemented by plain wooden tables and white walls. With shutters open and windows repaired, replaced or cleaned, subtle light flowed through. The 84-seat cinema, the Bellingham Film Palace, is there, too, along with five creative spaces on the previously derelict upper floor, managed by Lewisham Music, the Borough's music education service.

As always when working class pubs are reinvented, you have to ask yourself if it feels like gentrification. There were certainly some hipster signifiers here: pinboard menus, vintage chairs, flowery wallpaper, and so on. But there were also reassuring indications that a balance might have been found. In local accents, the staff discussed the hangovers they'd acquired after an appearance by a local reggae DJ in the function room the night before. And on the bar, alongside American-style IPA and cask ale, were Guinness and Stella Artois – pointed gestures of normality. As we sat in a quiet corner on a weekday lunchtime, Ernest Selley's 1927 account came to mind:

The dining room, like the whole of the interior, is panelled in unstained oak. There were only two others besides myself. Later on a woman who looked like a health visitor came in and sat at a table which was laid for one. She was evidently a regular customer. I ordered the one-and-sixpenny table d'hôte lunch. It was quickly served, hot, well-cooked and good value for money.

Substitute mac-and-cheese for the *table d'hôte lunch* and, yes, Ernest – same, even across those 90-odd years.

1926
The Angel*

Hillingdon, UB4 8HX

Improved Pubs appeared throughout London, but the most conspicuous examples were in suburban areas where there was the space to spread out and provide a fuller range of facilities. The architectural character of Improved Houses was often criticised for being bland but the Angel, designed by Thomas Nowell Parr for Fuller's Brewery in 1926, makes something special out of polite ingredients with Arts and Crafts-influenced joinery and Neo-Georgian proportions. A full Art Deco Masonic Lodge exists in the first floor club room. Nationally listed in 2015, the pub was sold by Fuller's in 2018 and is currently empty.

1930
The Black Lion

Hammersmith and Fulham, W6 9TJ

Independent member of parliament and novelist Alan Patrick Herbert's *The Water Gypsies* (1930) captures the Thames at Hammersmith and the canal inland from Brentford at a crucial moment, when waterways were fading as industrial spaces and itinerant canal workers faced hard choices over whether to move on to the land. The novel's hero, Jane is one such 'water gypsy' whose mooring is the Thames at Hammersmith and 'home from home' on dry land is the Black Swan pub facing the river, where a climactic (and skillfully-written) game of skittles takes place against the neighbouring pub, the Pigeons. The Black Swan – real name the Black Lion – recently reinstated its skittles alley making it one of a tiny handful of London pubs to play the game. The rival pub, the Pigeons, is also a lightly fictionalised version of the Dove, another notable riverside pub nearby.

Overleaf: Alan Patrick Herbert swings into action, 1938
© Lordprice Collection / Alamy Stock Photo

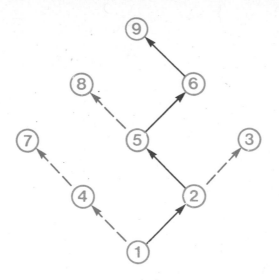

DIRECTION OF THROW

– – – – ▶ PATH OF FALLING SKITTLES

⸻▶ PATH OF CHEESE

A 'floorer'

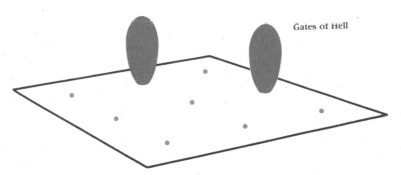

Gates of Hell

Knock on with a closed cheese high on the outside of either pin.

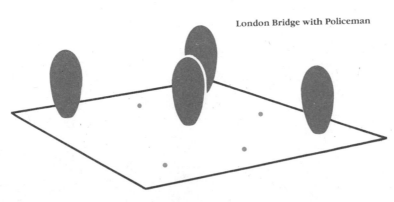

London Bridge with Policeman

Impossible in one shot.

1933

The Ace of Spades*

Kingston upon Thames, KT6 5AT

The Roadhouses that arrived in Britain in the late 1920s and early 1930s were a US import but quickly cross-bred with English Inn traditions, gaining gables, Mock-Tudoring and thatched roofs in the process. Sited at key motor junctions on new arterial roads, they combined petrol filling stations with 24-hour restaurants, bars, late night dance halls and, in the case of Kingston's Ace of Spades, even a swimming pool and aerodrome. The spirit of the place – a beauty show and a dance party in full swing – was captured on film by British Pathé in 1933. Combining the modernity and romance of the automobile with the English vernacular, the new possibilities and freedoms these Roadhouses represented must have provided a powerful high even before the champagne corks popped. Now almost entirely swept away, they feel impossibly out of reach.

Right: Advertisement in a theatre programme, 1932 © Alamy

1930

The Atlas

Kensington and Chelsea, SW6 1RX

Truman's Brewery pub interiors of the 1930s had a plain, rational and highly-crafted aesthetic which used light timber panelling, matchboarding, dainty brick-and-tile fireplaces and obscured lighting. The Atlas is one the best preserved examples of the Truman way in London, and has one extraordinary detail among all the good taste: a black and white checkerboard spittoon, designed to receive spittle and fag butts, running the length of the bar.

Below: Joy Mulandi

1937

The Earl Beatty

Merton, KT3 6JF

Neal Shasore

In 1936, the first world war naval commander, Admiral of the Fleet, David Beatty, First Earl Beatty died. Second in distinction only to John Jellicoe, he had played a critical role in the Battle of Jutland, and had before that built a reputation on his aggressive imperialist interventions in the Mahdist War and Boxer Rebellion. At the time of his death, he was held in such high esteem that the Prime Minister of the day, Stanley Baldwin, proposed a public memorial to honour him. Edwin Lutyens's new fountains for the quatrefoil basins in Trafalgar Square were dedicated to Jellicoe and Beatty respectively, and the two men were further commemorated with busts and engraved tablets nearby.

That was the realm of high art and public memorials. But perhaps inspired by Baldwin's tribute, Beatty was also honoured – in time-old fashion for military commanders – by having a pub named after him. Quick off the mark was Watney Combe & Reid, then the leading London brewery, who dubbed one of their new, sizeable suburban pubs, designed by their in-house architect, Alfred W. Blomfield, 'The Earl Beatty'. Opened in 1937, it was sited in Motspur Park, a suburban village off the Kingston bypass, within the old Merton and Morden Urban District. Motspur Park was – it still is – a quintessential suburban ribbon development of the interwar years: row after row of Tudoresque and Neo-Georgian semi-detached housing, corrupting the forms of the Garden Suburb built by John Innes nearby at Merton Park and the London County Council's St Helier Estate towards Morden.

Development of Motspur Park was opened up in part by the railways but it was also a product of the construction of the arterial road now known as the A3, which had a significant morphological impact on the local area. Both of these factors must have made the prospect of a new Improved Public House here an attractive one to Watney's – the Earl Beatty sits opposite the station, and not far from Shannon Corner on the A3. Typologically, therefore, it falls somewhere between a Roadhouse and a suburban Tavern with a large garden and parking area.

I grew up in Motspur Park. For all of my childhood, the Earl Beatty's pub sign featured a generic scene of Nelsonian naval warfare – all bicorn and billowing sails. A precocious local historian, I was never much convinced. Though Napoleonic in stature, Beatty was very much a 20th century Admiral, and often photographed with his cap set at a jaunty angle, his trademark 'Beatty tilt'.

The strange anachronism of the pub sign might seem a minor detail, but it reveals so much about interwar suburbia. It invites almost the suspension of disbelief at the Neo-Georgian architecture, and imagines instead an authentically Georgian past in Motspur Park, a place-name deliberately evocative of a medieval past (the 'Mots' were, supposedly, a local family with a 'furze' or gorse farm, and Motsfurze Farm was corrupted over time to 'Motspur Park'). It tells us about a need for an invented, deeper history by trading on ahistorical nostalgia.

But the contrivance of the Earl Beatty pub sign as I knew it half a century after its opening, was not an original one. In fact, when Watneys built their new pub at Motspur Park, people were taking pub signage rather more seriously.

To understand why, we need to turn to the Improved Public House movement (p72) which gave form to interwar pub design. Threatened by the enduring strength of the Temperance lobby and by government experiments in state control and design from 1916 onwards (notably the Carlisle Experiment in which the civil service took over hundreds of pubs, redesigning facades, interiors and menus to promote sobriety), brewers of the interwar period sought to 'improve' their pubs and Taverns to make them more salubrious and appeal to a wider demographic. Inspired by Redfern's 'New Model Inn' and the Arts and Crafts vernacular and Neo-Georgian forms deployed by

David Beatty, First Earl Beatty, while serving as Vice Admiral and sporting the 'Beatty tilt', portrait by John Buchan, 1916.

his team, the spaces and material culture of the pub was subsumed into the wider design reform movement. Architects began to take a keen interest.

The expanding suburban fringes of London, and the growth in private motor vehicle ownership led to the establishment of many large Improved Public Houses and Roadhouses (p80), with generous beer gardens and car parking spaces close to major arterial roads, serving the ribbon developments of new middle-class housing, sold on easy terms, often near to light industry. Watneys participated in this shift with some relish, developing their suburban presence significantly. The Earl Beatty is an archetypal example.

An often-forgotten byproduct of the Improved Public House was the 'Inn-sign revival'. As *Country Life* commented in 1930, brewers had 'been content to paint on a sign the name of the inn with the brand of ale to be obtained at it'. Since the war, however, the sign-painters' craft had been revived through the energies of craftspeople like Ralph Ellis, responsible for a number of signs in Sussex and Hampshire, and Ernest Michael Dinkel. Both had been engaged under the Carlisle Experiment. There were other centres of revival, noted by Basil Oliver: in Cambridgeshire, West Suffolk and especially Colchester in Essex. Oliver reflected that 'There is at least one firm of brewers, trading in East Anglia, who are systematically reforming all their sign-writing with the aid of the large-scale sheets… of lettering designed by Mr Eric Gill' in collaboration with Denis Tegetmeieir, which were available for purchase at the photograph stall of the V&A.

1936 – the year of Beatty's death – was a significant milestone in the 'Inn-sign revival'. Under the auspices of the Building Centre, the CPRE (then the Council for the

Preservation of Rural England) and the Brewers Society mounted an Inn-sign exhibition, held at the Centre's fashionable address at New Bond Street. Its organising committee included Edwin Lutyens, Albert Richardson and Basil Oliver, all leading figures in the revival of pubs and Inns after the first world war. Lutyens's much-praised 1934 Drum Inn in Cockington, Devon, had a sign painted by Laura Knight; Richardson, one of the leading advocates of the Georgian revival, had valorised the pub in *The English Inn, Past and Present: A Review of its History and Social Life* in 1925; Oliver, a scion of the Greene King brewing dynasty, had worked on the Carlisle Experiment. The exhibition – though tied into rural revivalism and a kind of parochial nostalgia – was nevertheless a celebration of a typically English Romantic Modernism. Richardson, in the introduction to the exhibition catalogue, called for more contemporary themes, hopeful that 'the Inn-signs of the future will represent the natural feelings of every walk of society. There is an opportunity to record national reactions to great events, political and historical, satirical and profound'. Richardson was not alone in his concern, as the *Times* reflected, there was a growing feeling that pub signs 'should be painted with subjects of modern interest… No one knows nowadays who the Marquess of Granby was, nor even that the sign painters of the past liked him as much for his bald head as for his gallantry in the field and his generous care for his men. Statesmen fall out of fashion even quicker than soldiers'. Instead, as correspondents suggested, tongue-in-cheek names and signs should reflect modern life, in particular the emerging 'carscape' of rural and suburban England: The Car and Starter, The Plug and Throttle and The Gudgeon Pin. Indeed *The Builder* insisted that the Inn-sign 'has today a greater significance in view of the growth of motor traffic. A sign which is attractive and maybe clearly distinguished at a distance is an essential in this age of rapid transport, for it is indicative of the tempo of modern life that motorists seldom turn back, and if they do not receive sufficient notice of an Inn before arriving at it, they will go on to the next'.

The Inn-signs exhibition was an unexpected success, seen by 18,000 visitors in its first month of opening. Of the 429 exhibits, a number came from the Carlisle Experiment as well as from leading London brewers, including Watneys. Artists included established names like Dinkel and Ellis, but there were also, notably, a number of women artists represented including Cicely Hey, Gertrude Hermes, Herry Perry, Estella Canziani, and Lady Sybil Grant, who produced an electrical sign. A number of designs were three-dimensional: Hermes's was a carved sign for the Myllet Arms in Perivale, and the sign for the Eight Bells, Watford, comprised a wrought iron frame incorporating ringing bells.

The exhibition led to the establishment of a register of artists and designers which pub owners and operators could consult, further stimulating the trade. The brewers responded with enthusiasm: Greene King Brewery commissioned a number of painted signs by Dinkel, produced on Plymax (copper-faced plywood), framed and glazed, with outlets for condensation, that were considered particularly successful. For Frederick Leney, a subsidiary of Whitbread Brewery, artists were commissioned to produce an original design, enlarged and transcribed onto metal sheets which were then painted. As the sign weathered, less skilled artists could 'restore its pristine freshness of colour… following the colour guide and the easily traced lines on the metal'. 350 signs for Kentish pubs were painted using this model. Watneys, the owners

Above: Cicely Hey, ink and
watercolour designs, c.1936.
Courtesy Abbott and Holder

Overleaf: Signs which
featured in the exhibition by
Ernest Dinkel, Ralph Ellis
and H. R. Hoskins

of the Earl Beatty, also employed reputable sign-painters; Ralph Ellis produced signs for a number of Surrey and London pubs including the Cricketers in Hale, the White Hart at Cranleigh, the Marquis of Granby in Esher, and the Earl Haig Hotel at Hounslow. It is perfectly feasible that he may have produced the original, now lost, sign for the Earl Beatty.

If the New Model Inns and the Improved Public Houses they led to demonstrated what architects could bring to the space of the pub, the Inn-sign revival showed how architects and their clients increasingly sought to extend the reach of design reform to the wider material culture of drinking and victualling. The Inn-sign revival was quickly followed, with a degree of almost absurd quaintness, by the Ale Garland revival in 1937; at the George Inn (p26) a garland of 'evergreens and winter berries' – the traditional trade sign of the innkeeper – was hung from a 'stake pushed through the rails' of its famous wooden gallery. In the same year, Whitbread organised an exhibition at the New Burlington Galleries of 'paintings, photographs, architectural designers, Inn-signs and other material with a view to showing the contribution of art to the civilizing of licenced premises'. The Central Institute of Art and Design (CIAD) initiated a scheme with four London brewers (Barclay Perkins, Courage, Watneys and Whitbread) entitled *Londoners' England* in 1944, to display paintings in their pubs, as a kind of travelling exhibition, 'part of a movement to bring the arts to the pub'. In 1948, CIAD and the brewers again collaborated on an Inn crafts exhibition at the Royal Society of British Artists Gallery in London; it represented, in the words of *the Architects' Journal*, a 'combined effort by British brewers to give help and encouragement to the traditional hand crafts of this country'. The exhibition was designed by Robert Gooden and Robert Russell (who later designed the Lion and Unicorn Pavilion at the Festival of Britain) and included specially designed glassware for Trust Houses and an elbow chair by David Pye, as well an Inn-sign by Michael Farrar Bell.

This intersection of design, craft and architecture with the spaces and material culture of the public was bound up in a wider cultural nostalgia, both of the rural and the urban which met in the distinct interwar suburban condition. Today, we could conceive of a more critical nostalgia for contemporary Inn craft, or at least a set of critical design and creative strategies to enliven the London pub after the dec-imation of the hospitality sector by the pandemic. This critical nostalgia could be playful and inclusive, rather than patrician and moralising and it could create oppor-tunities for collaboration with the creative arts and design as society emerges into a 'new normal'. Let's take the Earl Beatty – David Beatty was essentially an imperial war hero, and the last year has seen some of the dangers of inscribing towns and cities with the names of so-called 'great' men, like Edward Colston, Cecil Rhodes, even Winston Churchill. Could a revival of Inn craft instead form part of a process of reinscribing the city and its suburbs with new, more inclusive collective memory and invented tradition? The promoters of the Building Centre's exhibition were less interested in fixing the pub in aspic, but instead in reviving and reimagining drink-ing culture – the puns and language play, the invention of new rituals, the reflection of contemporary life, the collaboration between architecture and craft.

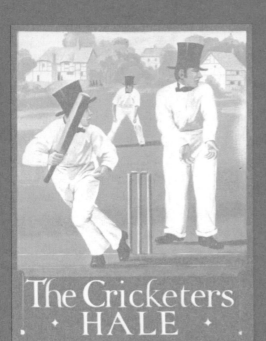

THE KING'S HEAD

The Cricketers
· HALE ·

The GREYHOUND

RICHMOND ARMS

EN·LA·ROSE·JE·FLEURIS

THE SPOTTED COW

3
KKKK

The Hampshire Hog

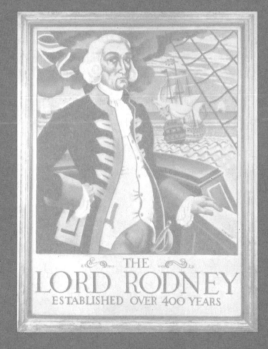

THE
LORD RODNEY
ESTABLISHED OVER 400 YEARS

1938

The Eastbrook

Barking and Dagenham, RM10 7UP

Between 1921 and 1935 the London County Council built 26,000 homes on the Becontree Estate, former market gardens between Barking and Dagenham. The estate included no less than 25 schools but, influenced by the Temperance movement and paternalistic ideas of the 'deserving poor', enforced a cap of six pubs. It was no surprise then, when in 1937 G. A. Smith & Dunning built an absolutely enormous Improved Pub on one of the main roads east of the estate. It survives today in remarkably original condition and retains its expansive 'music room', decorated with stained glass instruments at the windows. To the early residents of Becontree the Eastbrook must have been as far from the street corner locals of the East End as they could imagine but alluring all the same. It remains so today, a grandiose Neoclassical gesture in the midst of one of the world's most significant public housing estates.

Reem Albayati, Liam Andrews, Amy Ford, Dimitris Karaiskakis, Imeshka Ranatunga, Yannis Timagenis (2012)

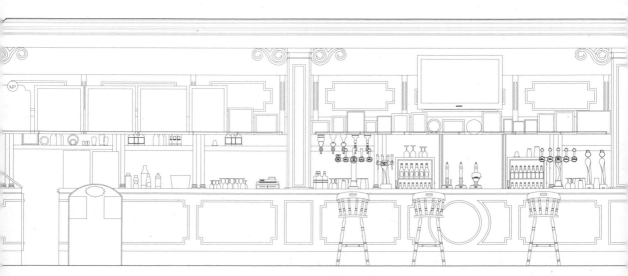

1938

The Windermere

Brent, HA9 8QT

Dutch Courage, we suppose, was the intended joke. The Improved Pubs movement of the 1920s and 1930s gave anonymous brewery architects an extraordinary chance to experiment in London's growing suburbs. In this case, the Courage Brewery built, at a heroic scale, a neo-Georgian brick palace with expressive Dutch gables and a Modernist-inflected interior. The distinctive ceramic fire surrounds inside are decorated with windmill motifs in another reference to the Netherlands. The pub has been telling passing train travellers to 'TAKE COURAGE' in enormous golden lettering on its facade since 1938.

1938

The Doctor Johnson*

Redbridge, IG5 0ES

The Doctor Johnson was built in 1937–8 for the Southwark-based Barclay, Perkins & Co. Brewery to the designs of H. Reginald Ross. A substantial roadhouse with multiple bars, a separate 'off-sales' pavilion and a huge garden, it was built as part of the wave of 1930s commercial optimism that accompanied abortive proposals to transform Fairlop Airfield into an international airport, and to serve the vast acres of new housing then being built in the area. The pub's exterior combines Neo-Georgian stylings with Art Deco horizontal geometry. The interior survives intact but tucked away behind the shelves of a Co-op supermarket.

1940
The Palm Tree

Tower Hamlets E3 5BH

When the Palm Tree was built in 1935 for Truman's it was an inconsequential street corner pub in a sea of Victorian terraces. After heavy bombing during the 1940 London blitz it was one of the few buildings left standing. Postwar, it was for a while surrounded by emergency prefabricated bungalows. Thanks to the institutional power of Church and Brewery, pubs and churches were often the only buildings untouched by postwar reconstruction and clearance projects (Rachel Whiteread's 1993 sculpture *House*, which stood nearby, commemorated this process) and the Palm Tree accordingly now sits alone and romantic in the middle of Mile End Park. While the change around the Palm Tree has been remarkable, the change inside is negligible. Its long history of saloon bar singalongs was captured in *The Last of the Crooners*, a 2018 photography exhibition by Tom Oldham and an accompanying LP of American jazz standards recorded live at the pub. Among the performers is acclaimed pianist Jack Honeyborne, who played with Vera Lynn for 20 years and appeared nude as part of an eight-piece band in the 1964 Pink Panther film, *A Shot in the Dark*.

1940
Skehans

Lewisham, SE14 5TW

On the night of 30 September 1940 a bomb landed on Evelina Road, Nunhead, knocking out every window of St Thomas the Apostle Roman Catholic Church and badly damaging its presbytery. As a result the clergy moved their regular mass to the function room of Duke of Albany in nearby Kitto Road, in a striking coming-together of church and pub. Nowadays known as Skehans, the pub has lost its mass but retains a committed congregation of regulars who value its sense of community and frequent music evenings. When the pub reopened in April 2021 for external drinking, the band turned up to play on-street.

Above: Tom Loughlin

The Travellers Friend

Redbridge, IG8 OPN

The Travellers Friend has stood on Woodford Green since 1841, initially as a Beerhouse only. It has retained, though no longer in their original location, a series of 'snob screens' which were designed to allow well-heeled customers to drink at the bar without having to look at the bar staff – a uniquely English invention. It was known as the Spivs during the second world war when it became renowned locally as a spot to acquire and trade contraband goods. Presumably the screens then allowed the bar staff to not look at what certain customers were up to.

1946

The Bride of Denmark*

Westminster, SW1H 9DP

A bar built in the basement of 9-13 Queens Anne's Gate, the offices of the Architectural Press, then one of the most influential espousers of Modernist architecture. The proprietor, Hubert de Cronin Hastings, observed the destruction of pubs during and after the London blitz and began organising for fragments to be relocated to his basement, including half a stuffed lion contributed by legendary architecture writer Nikolaus Pevsner. The result was a dark, claustrophobic and spatially-rich private club for London's architects from 1946 until it was shamefully dismantled and sold off in 1991. The Bride remains a brilliant conceit: an elusive, shadowy and very Victorian space created in the heart of progressive British architectural culture, where visiting luminaries including Frank Lloyd Wright would sign their names on a mirror with a diamond-tipped stylus. Three years after it was built, a special *Inside the Pub* issue of *the Architectural Review* appeared; a study of pubs as an architectural type that called for a rebooting of pub aesthetics in reaction to Brewer's Tudor, Improved Public houses and their like.

Right: © John Maltby / RIBA Collections. Overleaf: One of a selection of drawings made by Gorden Cullen for *the Architectural Review* special issue of October 1949.

COFFEE RO

The City of Quebec

Westminster, W1H 7AF

Paul Flynn

I first met Sam Lock in 1995, while working for a small magazine in Manchester. The book reviews pile sat on a corner shelf. One day early into my tenure, my editor said, 'pick a book and write me 350 words on it.' I leafed through the opening pages of five advanced proofs before locating Sam's debut novel *As Luck Would Have It*, to be published just after his 70th birthday. I fell in love with Sam right there and then.

The story is of a two-man flat-share in interwar Chelsea, one domineering monster and another gentler young soul radicalising himself to the sophisticated peculiarities of a new life in London. The opening page details a man dressed in women's clothes walking through the neighbourhood, noticing his appearance with stout, unhurried, quizzical admiration. Not long after reading him, I interviewed Sam in his studio apartment on the top floor of a municipal housing block at the football end of the Kings Road.

I'd never met a gay man his age before. He told me that he had not long since lost his lover of almost 40 years. Having mostly been in relationships lasting the approximate length of a haircut, this sole fact blew my mind. A friendship grew, filled with a casual transference of information, knowledge and taste across our generations, right up until the last time I saw Sam alive, 21 years after meeting, at the Chelsea and Westminster Hospital. I mention him not because it is approaching the fifth anniversary of his death but, more selfishly, because of the way he quietly transformed my life, providing it some new parameters of possibility.

Sam was the first man to take me to the City of Quebec, an unheralded gay pub tucked down a back alley off Oxford Street, just before Marble Arch. If Sam was the almanac from which I needed to learn, the Quebec became the stage on which to recite it. On the ground floor, the pub was not much distinguishable from a local Wetherspoons, though no-one at the chain would have either the wit or imagination to have dreamed up its core clientele: older gay men and their admirers, all of whom referred to it, mostly affectionately, as 'The Elephant's Graveyard.'

Down a creaking staircase in the middle of the room on Fridays, Saturdays and Sundays, like some rabid fever dream, or perhaps an imaginary David Lynch film starring Kenneth Williams, the unusual polarities of the Quebec's constituent drinkers sprang magically into life. The lighting was dim downstairs, with a small patch of discernible dancefloor illuminated by hard blue and red rotating bulbs. It was the sort of pub which suited a thick crust of cigarette smoke. There always seemed to be someone in there who knew the gay Kray twin. Chatty, horny, wise, funny, loose men across the generations would swap eye contact, phone numbers and conversational *bon mots* accrued from their years of service to the gay social cause. At the extravagantly long latrines in the Gents' at the furthest recess of the pub's basement, they would sometimes share more. The Quebec reminded me a little of working men's clubs back home, if the men frequenting them wore pocket squares and gossiped about the waiting staff at The English National Opera.

Over many years as a *habitué* of the Quebec, I attuned to its frankness and colour, chaos and sense, plural singularity. I was always slightly off kilter there, because I came for the stories not the sex. Three pints in, it hardly mattered. As a young man, I sometimes caught the wandering eye of a storied fellow but as I turned middle-aged, I entered the invisible quotient at neither end of its scales of attraction. As he floated from his 70s to his 80s as a newly celebrated author, Sam was quite the hit.

I was an early starter with gay pubs, lucky enough to like their waspish flavour from the start of my journey through them, one of the benefits of coming of age in a city like Manchester where everybody knows everybody else and you can ease yourself into their fresh rhythms in three weeks flat. I schooled myself in the busy strip of gay bars along the Rochdale Canal, then for a five-year spell as a student across Glasgow, a rougher, readier, less amplified version of the same thing. By my mid-20s I'd drunk in gay bars in New York, Milan, Paris and Berlin, each pint peeling back a thin but nonetheless revelatory layer of the city's skin. But nothing prepared me for the obdurate strangeness of the City of Quebec, a bustling new masonic lodge of geron-tophilia. Sometimes when I look back at first stepping into the place, I wonder whether it wasn't my deciding factor in eventually moving to London. You wouldn't find a place like the Quebec anywhere else on earth.

That mix of the old and the new filled a knowledge gap no university qualification could hope to plug. It reversed everything I'd learned about gay men's obsession with youth and populated the invisible space of the generation who preceded mine, one ravaged by AIDS. I loved the way it tampered with my preconceptions of what a gay life might look like. It prepared me in a round-about way for my 30s, then 40s. This year I will turn 50. Before long, I'll be greyer and slower and attractive once again to the denizens of the Quebec, a rite of passage I'd never have conceived of had I not been led by the hand of a brilliant man into this brilliant pub. In my mind, still, the Quebec is indistin-guishable from Sam. The taps we drank from lubricated a special friendship, one which is further indistinguishable from the way I see London and what I choose to take from it. This is what the Quebec is there for.

I moved to London with two fixed ideas about the city; that it was preposterously expensive but ultimately worth the pay-out. By now I had a job at a daily newspaper with an editor I recognised from the TV. What would life look like under these elevated circumstances? I thought, wrongly, that London's appeal would spill out of its worldly privilege and prestige. I imagined – pah! – that I might enjoy fancy private member's clubs, before remembering that in Manchester you learn by instinct that the party starts not when you keep the riff raff out, but when you fling back the doors and invite them in. I thought I would sit impervious at lacquered bars sipping variants of coffee from chrome machines the North had never heard of while perusing European newspapers. Maybe I would meet a man named Troy. In all these anticipatory thoughts, I'd quite forgotten that moving cities means your circumstance changes while you remain essentially the same.

Once that idea settled, London focused itself into the pleasingly cracked picture emerging from a complicated jigsaw puzzle. The hunt for missing Quebec-type pieces began in earnest. It turned out the city had plenty of niche up its sleeve, the key separation factor in distinguishing it from the provinces. There was something battered, chipped and bruised about its best hostelries, gay and straight. This war-torn element came as a surprise but suited my disposition. I spent Wednesdays crossing the 50 footsteps from the Old Ship in Limehouse – a vessel of kitschy maritime memorabilia, nominally credited as London's oldest gay pub – to an amateur strip night at the White Swan, a big disco pub favoured by lairy Essex interlopers as fit and hungry as butcher's dogs. Sundays in Soho was karaoke at the bear pub, the Kings Arms, crackling with warmth and bonhomie to the strains of burly, hirsute men singing David Bowie songs. A trio of pubs close to my address off the Hackney Road turned gay, first the Joiners Arms,

then the George and Dragon (see The Queen Adelaide, p180) and the Nelson's Head. They all smelled of mischief, oddness and decay, tracing a line from the wild experimentalism of beguiling young fashion students trying on new identities for size, and the wisdom of their forebears who'd long since found theirs. The one anchor that kept me moored to London's not quite under, not quite overworld was always the Quebec.

There is not a word, I believe, for the sensation of disquiet and comfort caused by entering a favourite pub of a favourite person just after they have died. For my first visit after Sam's passing in 2016, I went alone, to gauge how that might feel. Because of the nature of the Quebec, perhaps because of its mainstay drinkers' comfortably worn relationship with their age, it fit like a pair of old slippers.

Pubs are not roundly regarded as places of wholesome recuperation and reflection. Quite the opposite. An old drunk once cocked his head at me from the length of a bar and scolded: 'whatever answers you're looking for, you won't find at the bottom of that glass'. As I scrolled through old photos of Sam on my phone, reconciling myself to the absence of the man who'd laid open a pathway for gay life beyond my immediate sightline, those words came creeping back. He may well have been right. In which case, I had better order another.

1949
The White Hart*

Hillingdon, TW6 2AA

In March 1949 Ken Colyer, a carriage cleaner on the London Underground, secured the weekly use of a hut beside the White Hart in Cranford for rehearsals of his quartet, the Crane River Jazz Band. Though the name sounds straight out of New Orleans, the Crane is actually the Thames tributary that ran alongside the pub and gave Cranford its name. The rehearsals quickly became a hugely popular jazz club. A feature of the night was a reduced three-piece 'breakdown band' to play in gaps between full band performances, mainly covers of black American musicians like Lead Belly and Big Bill Broonzy. This was the birth of skiffle, a DIY musical style that inspired a generation of teenagers (John Lennon and Paul McCartney among them) to pick up a guitar, washboard or washtub bass. The venue that gave the space for this pivotal stage in the history of Rock and Roll was demolished in 2010 and is now a drive-through KFC on the fringes of Heathrow Airport, but the Crane river still flows alongside, on its way to New Orleans.

1951
The French House

Westminster, W1D 5BG

It is drenched in legends of bohemian debauchery. It's got a Dylan Thomas anecdote. It has peculiar, inexplicable rules (no pints, only halves). It has an acclaimed former 'guvnor', Gaston Berlemont, who was born upstairs and ran the pub with generosity and charisma for decades (from 1951 to 1989). It was designed by an acclaimed and prolific 'brewery architect', Alfred W. Blomfield. But The French House's greatest claim to posterity is that it manages to be the definitive Soho boozer and also profoundly cosmopolitan, French, obviously, but also properly international in spirit, a meeting place for anyone passing through the city who wants their visit to be derailed, a local for strangers and travellers, an entry point into a kind of Soho nightlife that otherwise seems to exist only in literary biographies of the long-dead. Now in the hands of Lesley Lewis for over 30 years, it continues to be excellent.

Gaston Berlemont holding court behind the bar, 1950s
© Bridgeman Images

1953

The Kenilworth Castle*

Kensington and Chelsea, W11 4BU

Following bomb damage during the Blitz,
and in line with practice across London,
substantial areas of North Kensington
were redeveloped to provide municipal
public housing in place of often-crumbling
19th century speculative development.
Henry Dickens Court, named after the local
Alderman and grandson of the famous
author, was one of the first housing projects
to appear, completing in 1953. A pub was
proposed as part of the masterplan, and
The Kenilworth Castle was the first thing
built on the site, to designs by architect
F. W. Handover which have more in common
with Charles Holden's visionary interwar
Tube stations than they do with conventional
pub design. Always a popular local pub,
the Kenilworth closed in 2014 and is now
a supermarket.

© Architectural Press Archive / RIBA Collections

1956

The Lord Nelson

Southwark, SE1 0LR

The Lord Nelson is one of the few remaining purpose-designed Estate Pubs in central London. Nelson Square was a grand 19th century square that was severely damaged during the London blitz. Southwark Council and architects Sydney Clough, Son & Partners planned a scheme to house 1,300 people on the site, retaining the grassy square at the centre but replacing the houses with apartment blocks of heroic scale. At the base of the first, the Lord Nelson was built for Charrington Brewery, in the same red brick as the rest of the block but set forward in a public gesture with an exaggerated bow window facing a street terrace. A beer on that terrace still allows a sense of what the designers and civil servants intended, even if the art school student union aesthetic it pulls off today (and it does pull it off) must be quite far from those intentions.

Above: Courtesy National Brewery Heritage Trust
Left: Lucinda Rogers

1960
The Shakespeare's Head

Islington, EC1R 1XA

The Shakespeare's Head is a petite, precisely-detailed red-brick box sitting neatly on a quiet street corner. Opened in around 1960, the pub got stuck in the mid-1970s, which is a brilliant and, in the context of north Clerkenwell, very surprising thing. The Modernist interior is softened by postwar populism; a little light tongue and groove pine, a little heavy stone cladding. The pub acts as an unofficial theatre bar for Sadler's Wells just around the corner, and an interval bell rings in time with each evening's performance.

Below: © Historic England

1961
The Cavendish Arms

Lambeth, SW8 2HJ

The Cavendish was built around 1960 as part of the Lansdowne Green Estate on the Wandsworth Road to the designs of Arthur Kenyon, who had previously worked with Louis de Soissons on the design of housing for Welwyn Garden City. The architects and planners of the Garden City movement tended to also be Temperance advocates by inclination and so pubs (or at least ones serving alcohol) were not provided. Meanwhile, back in Lambeth, the Lansdowne retained an old pub as part of its design (now demolished) and provided a new one, the Cavendish – a humble pitched-roof brick box on a key pedestrian route through the estate. The pub's long-running *Comedy Virgins* night is an established open-mic night for new acts who perform on the basis that they bring a friend, guaranteeing a full room and at least one fan (unless it goes *really* badly) for every act.

1964

The Willoughby Arms

Kingston upon Thames, KT2 6LN

In 1964 the Willoughby's upstairs room was a regular rehearsal space for the Yardbirds, a pivotal band in the British rhythm and blues scene and later pioneers of psychedelia who, unlike the bluesmen who inspired them, were a product of the leafy suburbs. These days, blues and traditional folk music co-exist with some very large televisions and, on St. George's Day, Morris dancers.

1965

The Coach and Horses

Lambeth, SW9 8LN

In the 1950s and 1960s it was still common for London pubs to only allow black people in certain bars. One response to this segregation was the growth in informal drinking clubs and house parties aimed at a West Indian clientele, particularly concentrated in areas like Brixton where many Windrush generation immigrants had settled: Coldharbour Lane alone had five such clubs. Oliver 'George' Berry, born in Jamaica, went one further when he became London's first black licensee of a public house in 1965, taking on the Coach and Horses, also on Coldharbour Lane. Attracting a multicultural crowd to live music such as Chubby Mullins and his All Stars, Berry ran the pub for several decades, weathering a devastating firebomb attack in 1973 by the National Front. After his departure in the 1990s the building has been run under various guises none of which celebrate its story and place in history.

Left: Oliver 'George' Berry after the firebomb attack
Overleaf: Chris Steele-Perkins / Magnum Photos

1966
The Barley Mow

Westminster, W1U 6QW

'A real pub, a proper local' wrote Ian Nairn in 1966, and not much seems to have changed since. Nairn also appreciated the two booths situated against the bar which allow an extremely intimate and private drinking experience overlooked only by the bar staff. Perfect, in Nairn's words again, 'for romantic indiscretion or flogging atomic secrets.'

1969
The King's Head*

Havering, RM1 3ER

On 19 May 1969 – a school night – two teenagers, Chris Fenwick and Lee Collinson, took the train to Romford from their homes in Essex and made their way to the Kings Head, an ancient, deep-planned Inn that had for centuries provided lodgings, stabling and good times for the town's charter market. Though the Inn's big back room was used at times for civic engagements and formal dinners, tonight it was hosting Howlin' Wolf, the globally-celebrated Chicago bluesman. During the performance, which was aggressive, powerful and transcendent, Lee Collinson became Lee Brilleaux. He bought a harmonica the next day, formed a blues band based in the 'Thames delta' of Canvey Island, started wearing a filthy white suit on stage, and led his band Dr. Feelgood to huge fame and influence over the pub rock movement and, ultimately, punk. In a way the most surprising part of this story is that Howlin' Wolf, by then globally adored, was playing a back room in a Romford pub – a reminder that this network of function rooms played a vital role in the development of popular music, spreading ideas and energies in unpredictable directions.

KING'S HALL
ROMFORD MARKET
Monday, May 19th
HOWLIN'
WOLF

ROUNDHOUSE
LODGE AVE., DAGENHAM
Saturday, May 17th
Due to the unfortunate acci-
dent, a replacement for
FAIRPORT CONVENTION is
being negotiated.

DOORS OPEN 7.30 :: LICENSED BAR

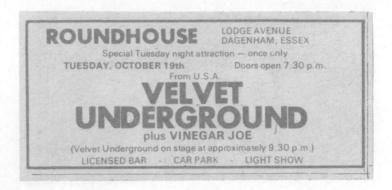

1969

The Roundhouse

Barking and Dagenham, RM8 2HY

The Village Blues Club, located in the former indoor bowling green of the Roundhouse pub on the western fringes of the huge London County Council Becontree Estate, had a shaky start and a tiny number of attendees despite booking acts like the newly-formed Led Zeppelin. In desperation, the club's promoters took a large number of half-price tickets to the Rolling Stones' free 1969 Hyde Park concert (estimated attendance between 250,000 and 500,000) and achieved an on-stage shout out from Mick Jagger. After that, the Roundhouse was mobbed for the next six years, becoming one of the definitive rock venues of London before noise complaints closed it down until a series of reunion events 37 years later. The pub would be remarkable even without its place in rock history though, for its unique circular plan with three first floor wings and a central rectangular turret – an extremely striking formal composition by Alfred Blomfield, otherwise known for more polite Neoclassical urban public houses like The French House (p102) and the Bedford Hotel (p117) in Balham.

Left: Barking and Dagenham Archive Photos / Egbert Smart Collection

1969
The Royal Standard

Croydon, CRO 1SS

For most of its existence the Royal Standard was an ordinary corner boozer in an area of tightly-knit Victorian terraces south-east of Croydon town centre. And in most respects it still is, run until recently for 25 years by local legend Martin 'Polly' Perkins, a reliable source of unadventurous but well-kept ale and a CAMRA stalwart. But in 1969 Croydon Council built the Croydon Flyover, a piece of a much larger planned road system and now a marooned fragment of heavy-duty raised concrete carriageway. The project wiped out a number of Victorian houses and a couple of pubs, but in due course provided the Standard with the most unusual beer garden in London: a small fenced-off area in the shadow of the enormous flyover. It's a unique spatial experience and we're still waiting for Suede to write a song about it.

1975
The Hole in the Wall

Lambeth, SE1 8SQ

Trendy bars colonising Victorian railway arches have become 21st century harbingers of London's gentrification, but the Hole the Wall is something older, weirder and more distinctive. If you get past the extraordinarily unwelcoming street frontage, directly facing the main entrance to Waterloo station, you'll find a two-barred pub built into a railway arch on its way to Charing Cross station. Apparently dating back to the 1930s, the pub has been a champion of real ale since it was an extremely niche activity in the early 1970s. Pubs at city rail termini have a particular quality, a local to nobody but depended on by many, and this is perhaps the ultimate London example of the type.

1979
The Golden Heart

Tower Hamlets, E1 6LZ

Sandra Esquilant and her husband Dennis became tenant landlords of the Golden Heart in 1979 when the freeholder, Truman's Brewery, was a large going concern one street away and Spitalfields Market was still providing London with its fresh fruit and vegetables directly opposite. Truman closed down its 11 acre site in 1989 and the market moved to Leytonstone in 1991 bringing a few lean years, but by then the area was already home to a multitude of artists and the Golden Heart quickly found a new and devoted clientele, among them Sarah Lucas, Tracey Emin and Gillian Wearing. Esquilant was subsequently named one of the 100 most influential people in the UK art world by *Art Review* magazine, and remains in charge of the Golden Heart, maintaining it as boisterous and unpredictable.

1977
The Hope and Anchor

Islington, N1 1RL

Pub rock predated and directly influenced punk, but didn't have the marketing department. This was DIY chic and razor blade earrings before such things went mainstream. The function rooms and pub basements of Greater London and Essex were the natural venue providing the intimacy, intensity, roughness and masculinity that the movement ran on. The pub in the name, if you had to pick one, would probably be the Hope and Anchor on Islington's Upper Street. Sweat dripped from the ceiling in 1977 when the month-long Front Row Festival featured performances from the Stranglers, X-Ray Spex, the Pirates and Dire Straits, and led to the release of a double live album. The basement of the Hope remains a venue.

SIDE 1
1. Dr. Feelgood **WILKO JOHNSON BAND**
2. Straighten Out **THE STRANGLERS**
3. Styrofoam **TYLA GANG**
4. Don't München It **THE PIRATES**
5. Speed Kills **STEVE GIBBONS BAND**
6. I'm Bugged **XTC**
7. I Hate School **SUBURBAN STUDS**

SIDE 2
1. Billy **THE PLEASERS**
2. Science Friction **XTC**
3. Eastbound Train **DIRE STRAITS**
4. Bizz Fizz **BURLESQUE**
5. Let's Submerge **X-RAY-SPEX**
6. Crazy **999**

SIDE 3
1. Demolition Girl **THE SAINTS**
2. Quite Disappointing **999**
3. Creatures of Doom **THE ONLY ONES**
4. Gibson Martin Fender **THE PIRATES**
5. Sound Check **STEEL PULSE**
6. Zero Hero **ROOGALATOR**

SIDE 4
1. Underground Romance **PHILIP RAMBOW**
2. Rock & Roll Radio **THE PLEASERS**
3. On the Street **TYLA GANG**
4. Johnny Cool **STEVE GIBBONS BAND**
5. Twenty Yards Behind **WILKO JOHNSON BAND**
6. Hanging Around **THE STRANGLERS**

Executive Production - Ian Grant and Clive Banks
Co-ordination - Jonathan Clyde

Many thanks to the following people without whom etc.
John Eichler, Tony Mann, Alan Edwards.

Recorded by RAK Mobile.

Engineered by Tim Summerhayes.

Sleeve concept and design - George Snow.

Mastered by George Peckham (Master Room).

A Warner Brothers Recording distributed by WEA Records Ltd. © 1978
A Warner Communications Company
Sleeve printed and made in England by
Gothic Print Finishers Ltd. London SE9 2EQ.

K66077.

1981

The Atlantic

Lambeth, SW9 8LQ

The Atlantic, as it was originally named and
as we will refer to it, made national headlines
in 1981 when it provided the backdrop to scenes
of rioting throughout Brixton whose significant
black community were disproportionately
affected by unemployment, poor housing, high
crime levels and institutional racism. The
Atlantic survived the riots unscathed despite
being at the epicentre of events thanks to
its long history as an informal community
centre to Brixton's West Indian population,
as described by *Flamingo* magazine in 1964.
Following a rebrand as the Dogstar and a shift
to a more affluent, mostly white crowd, the
pub was targeted in a later wave of riots in 1995
protesting the gentrification and white-washing
of the area. In 2016 the Atlantic signage was
reinstated in red embossed lettering on the
pub's prominent cornice.

Above: Police officers gather outside the Atlantic,
Kim Aldis, 1981.

1985

The Pride of Spitalfields

Tower Hamlets, E1 5LJ

The Pride opened in the middle of the 19th century as The Romford Arms, a backstreet Alehouse just outside the City of London and a few moments' walk from Spitalfields Market. Just around the corner is the Brick Lane Jamme Masjid, an 18th century building which before becoming a mosque in 1976 has also been – in reverse order – a synagogue, a Methodist chapel, a Wesleyan chapel and a Protestant chapel. The Pride, a tiny one-and-a-half room pub, must have welcomed a similarly diverse clientele over the years, though since its rename in the 1980s it has carefully avoided undue change to its interior and character. It's a time capsule of how London did ordinary pubs in the 1970s and 1980s: carpet, cats, red banquette seating, vinyl records playing and uproarious New Year's Eve celebrations involving nets of balloons hung from the ceiling. The Pride's walls host prints and photographs of London history and every couple of decades they get rearranged, but only slightly.

Below: Phillip Forde, Nelo Katodriti, Marina Popykarpou, Armin Sharifi (London Public House Project, 2012)

1983

The Bedford Hotel

Wandsworth, SW12 9HD

Alfred W. Blomfield, house architect of Watney Combe Reid & Co., managed to design three pubs with lasting cultural impact: The French House (p102), The Roundhouse (p112) and the Bedford Hotel. From the street an elegant but uneventful Neo-Georgian design on a prominent corner in Balham, the Bedford's claim to fame is its circular Club Room at the rear, an original 1931 design feature and, since 1983, home to the Banana Cabaret Comedy Club. Described by Stewart Lee as 'the best stand-up proving ground in the world', the list of British stand-ups who haven't performed at the Bedford feels shorter than the one of those who have.

1985

The Queen Victoria

Walford, E20

Rupa Huq

This essay explores the changing function and form of the suburban pub, using examples drawn from the London Borough of Ealing and a wider context of pubs found in popular culture. While we know that suburban pubs are suffering a decline in numbers, perhaps a stronger decline than in urban contexts, this is less a story of decline and more one of renewal and reinvention.

We all inhabit complex Venn diagrams. As a lifelong dweller in W5, Ealing (barring a couple of years away for study), this might qualify me as someone for whom the pub was a constant, but as a British Asian suburbanite, of Muslim background to boot, the pub was not a feature of my life growing up. The nearest parade of shops to our resolutely dry 1930s semi close to Hangar Lane tube had no watering holes. Instead my introduction to the pub came vicariously via television (and the opposite side of London): the Queen Vic on *EastEnders*, a place in which the whole neighbourhood of Albert Square, clientele bisecting class and gender, seemed to gather for a pint – from GP Dr Legg to the barrow boy market traders including Gita and Sanjay who most looked like me and mine.

While the pub was alive and well on the telly, the same narrative of decline we now hear about pubs was applied to a range of other 'suburban mainstays', among them banks, cinemas and churches.

A memorable NatWest TV ad from 2001 depicts an elderly lady on an unsuccessful quest to do some everyday banking deflatedly declaring to camera, 'my bank is now a trendy wine bar'. The ad signaled the bank's intention of keeping its branches open in opposition to wider trends at the time, but seen from today's perspective this assurance seems extremely anachronistic. Locally, Barclays were the last bank standing in West Ealing and Acton, and they shut up shop in 2020 and late 2021 respectively. The loss of cinemas in earlier decades was blamed on the rise of television and we have also seen the number of churches shrinking in the face of secularisation and rising multiculturalism and multiple faiths. In turn, home entertainment and multiculturalism have also been blamed for shrinking pub numbers, plus the widespread availability of budget booze over the counter causing a shift to home drinking and a general reduction in how much we consume alcoholic drinks.

We know that pubs facilitate much more than just drinking and are important sites for social interaction, becoming focal points for gossip, culture and economy. Some of this interaction became exclusive and subcultural, with pubs becoming informal labour exchanges and illicit markets for the distribution of knock-off goods – class B substances, watches, tapes, DVD-Rs, as lovingly documented in the Nags Head of *Only Fools and Horses*. This exclusivity has also been shown to us on screen – pubs that are so integrated with their communities that they exclude strangers, such as in the 1981 hit *An American Werewolf in London* in which a tight clientele of rural locals greets two US backpackers suspiciously.

Later I too, as small brown woman, would find establishments deep in middle England would meet my entering and asking for a coffee with quizzical looks. Today's suburban pubs seem to have deliberately reacted against this intimidating insularity, ripping out heavy wood furniture and fittings just as suburban churches have done away with their pews in an effort to make places that are more inviting, adaptable and flexible. The dark, carpeted pub interiors of *Men Behaving Badly* or *Two Pints of Lager and a Packet of Crisps* were becoming anachronistic, nostalgic even, as the programmes broadcast.

Meanwhile, Ealing's pubs are developing in a number of different directions. Many are indeed being lost, with housing targets and a weakened planning system seeing them replaced with apartment buildings as we have witnessed at the Kings Arms on

Acton Vale. Others have been absorbed into chains: the 'trendy wine bar' Crispins on Ealing Broadway, which has been rebranded the Sir Michael Balcon, after the director famous for his work at Ealing Studios, and the Red Lion and Pineapple, both of which have been succumbed to the Wetherspoons tide. Others are simply having to work harder, it seems, to attract a clientele and deliver a unique offer – the former Redback on Acton High Street used to attract queues of young Australians, New Zealanders and South Africans lured by its 'drink as much as you like' offers, nowadays it is the Aeronaut, a ticketed pub offering circus, acrobatics burlesque and music hall. The latter of which would have been familiar to suburban pubs of a hundred years previously, in which music hall entertainment and the public bar often intermingled – a moment when the pub and popular culture were one and the same.

The minority ethnic populations of Ealing have helped to rejuvenate rather than kill the public house by combining more traditional public house uses with karahi grills and related cuisine, for example the Duke of Wellington and Prince of Wales (p143) in Southall, and other examples in Hounslow such as the African Queen (p175). In these contexts the 'ethnoburbs' – clusters of distinct ethnic grouping within suburbs – often have a stronger relationship to their local public houses than other suburban areas.

A final development, and a phenomenon which the suburbs are leading on, is the rise of the Microbrewery, Brewpub and Micropub. All three suggest a 'back to basics' ethos and are often combined under the same roof, bringing the pub right back to its origin. When the George and Dragon re-opened as a Brewpub in 2014 (first with the Dragonfly Brewery and latterly with Portobello), *Time Out* wrote of how the pub was 'pouring beers made on the premises, possibly for the first time in centuries'. At the other end of the constituency in W13, a childrens' bookshop, the Owl and Pussycat, ceased trading in 2013 before re-opening – with the same name – as Ealing's first Micropub three years later. Micropubs are not typically tied to a particular brewery and eschew gimmickry and music in favour of conversation and intimacy: almost like being in someone's living room. The square footage of the Owl and Pussycat is significantly smaller than established pubs like The Forrester or The Plough which sit at opposite ends of the same street, Northfield Avenue. Such micro establishments are booming in the suburbs particularly, and nearby Hanwell is now home to the Dodo Micropub (p190). Such places bring the pub's character back to that of the idealised Queen Vic or Rovers Return, an intense public room where the local community comes to speak together.

The suburban home, particularly the 1930s semi, is notable for its capacity to take on different stylings and adaptations in response to the whims and desires of its residents – car-ports, porches, crazy paving, conservatories and paved front gardens. As with the suburban semi, the suburban pub in places like Ealing has shown a capacity to evolve and adapt in response to changing times and changing ideas.

The pub's constant reimagining in Ealing as elsewhere shows that it is flexible enough to encompass continuity and change in suburbia, a story richer and more complex than the idealised narratives of the Queen Vic.

Set of the Queen Victoria, 2015 © BBC Archives

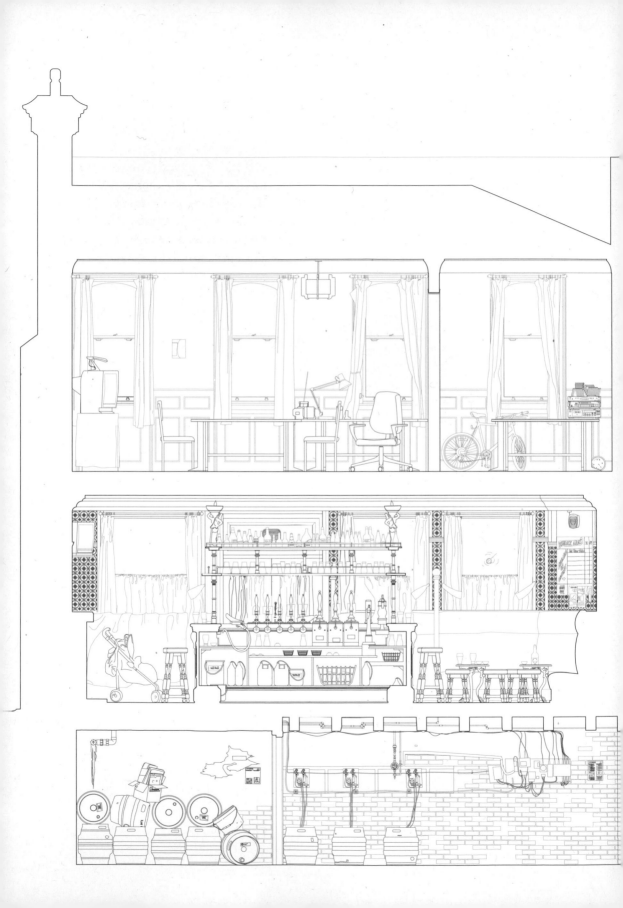

1994

The Wenlock Arms

Hackney, N1 7TA

Steve Barnes and J. R. 'Will' Williams walked into the Wenlock, a scruffy corner-pub off the City Road, in around 1994 and – two early retirement packages later – it was theirs. Their enthusiasms – Will's for trad jazz and Steve's for good beer – plus their skill as landlords in exercising just the right (lack of) control, plus the pub's context in the midst of light industrial sheds, Georgian townhouses and public housing estates, combined to create a place which became a home from home to an incredible diversity of regulars. In an increasingly atomised London, the Wenlock's island bar allowed everyone who crossed the threshold with an open heart to feel at home in the city. It was our living room for several years and served that role for many others too, acting as a daily reminder of why we gather and come together. The Wenlock birthed several bands, acted as a labour exchange for a range of businesses, fostered cricket and football teams, as well as a vibrant live music culture with regulars including the virtuoso jazz pianist Johnny Parker. Its upstairs function room was, among many other things, the meeting room of the British Stammering Association. Barnes and Williams moved on in 2011 and the pub remains lively and convivial, though, now surrounded by blocks of private residential new-build, its wilder years may be over.

Liidia Grinko, Ming-Kun Huang, Sharareh Khodabaksh, Mario Soustiel (2009–10)

1995

The Partridge

Bromley, BR1 IHE

Built in 1927 by architects Gunton & Gunton, the Partridge was for its first 70 years a branch of the National Provincial (latterly NatWest) Bank. As such its Classicism is a bit more sober, muscular and upright than the average 20th century Neoclassical pub. It takes some design cues from the 17th century Bromley College just up the road, and also handles its street corner position deftly, with a baroque bulge preserving the symmetry of the main elevation, which feels like a slightly over-grand urban townhouse. The pub is similarly grand inside, with a lofty, highly decorative main bar room that is certainly one of the best public interiors in Bromley.

1995

The Windmill

Lambeth, SW2 5BZ

The Windmill was built in 1971, a low-slung box on the edge of the Blenheim Gardens estate, an exemplary low-rise, high-density housing project designed by Lambeth Borough Architects Department under the direction of the influential architect and town planner Ted Hollamby (who also bought and restored William Morris' Red House in Bexleyheath). It would be interesting enough already as a surviving example of a Community Pub delivered as part of a postwar public housing development, but it has also been a hugely significant live music venue since the mid 1990s with a strong reputation for putting faith in some truly excellent emerging acts. This spirit returned in 2020 when a live album of recordings made at the Windmill was released as a lockdown fundraiser, featuring recordings by black midi, Lias Saoudi, Squid, Shame and Misty Miller among others, with funds split between the venue and Brixton Soup Kitchen.

Above: Childhood play the Windmill, @lousmithphoto

1995

The Harp

Westminster, WC2N 4HS

When Binnie Walsh took over the Harp in 1995 it was the latest in a string of pubs she and her husband Don had turned into something special. Among them was the postwar Albert Tavern in South Norwood, which they transformed into a Community Pub in the 1970s, providing a home for the Northwood Morris Men, a Scout troop, the local branch of the Labour Party and two cricket clubs. Walsh was also instrumental in getting real ale back at the bar and her belief in good beer reached a peak at the Harp, where the sheer number of customers gave her the chance to deliver a broad, deep and beautifully-kept ramp of beers and ciders. Over the years the community has campaigned to reopen the alleys and courts behind the pub as public spaces. Nowadays al fresco drinkers can choose between the street frontage – where the whole elevation opens up to serve as a bar counter – or the close-knit alleys behind, which also provide a handy entrance for employees of the adjacent Coliseum theatre. Binnie left the Harp when it was impossible to continue in 2014 and died in 2016.

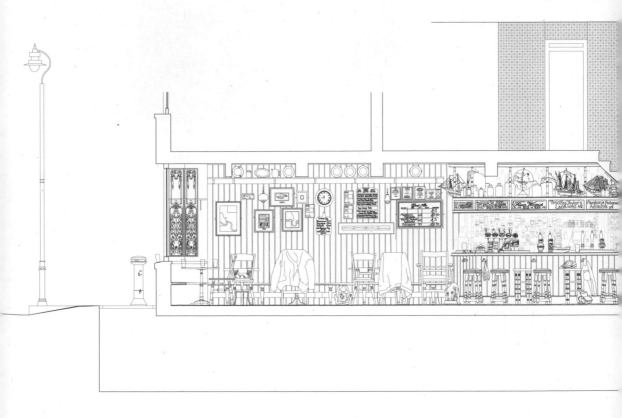

1995

The Grapes

Tower Hamlets, E14 8BP

Between 1995 and 2012 a visitor to the Grapes in Limehouse, travelling through along eerily quiet streets and between former warehouses around Limehouse Basin, might arrive at the pub's unassuming front door on Narrow Street and find it locked, with an A4 sheet of paper pinned to it bearing the Playboy logo. Within, away from the public's gaze, a reunion of former 'bunnies' would be underway, hosted by publican Barbara Haigh who had been a bunny herself before moving into the pub

trade. Scholars disagree on whether the Grapes was the model for the bleak, foggy Thameside pub in Dickens' *Our Mutual Friend*, but whatever the truth the Grapes retains the vibe of an edge-of-land Alehouse that faces the river as much as it faces the street. Haigh, who sold the pub to a group including actor Ian McKellen (who nowadays occasionally comperes the Grapes pub quiz), preserved the pub's archaic atmosphere but added a well-regarded fish restaurant upstairs.

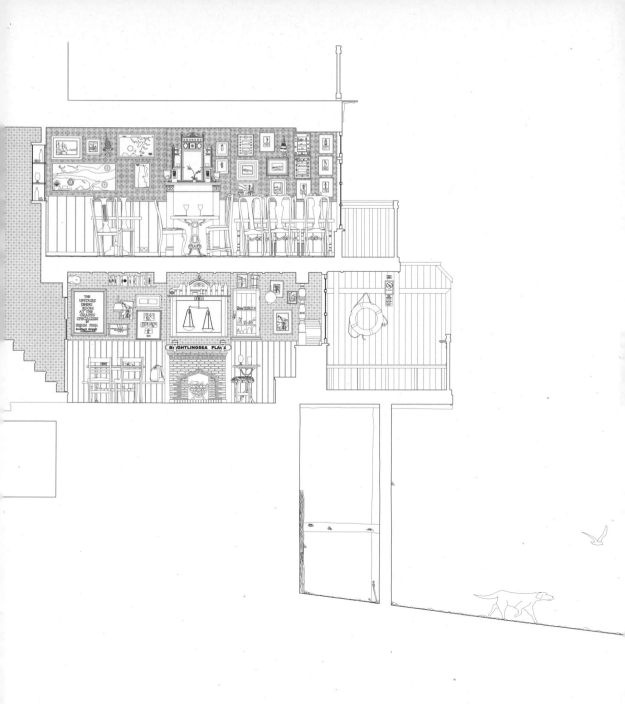

Alexandra Bailey, Carlos
Dos Santos, John Henden,
Thomas Sellers (2009–10)

The Jerusalem Tavern

Islington, EC1M 5UQ

Phineas Harper
David Knight
Cristina Monteiro
Daniel Rosbottom
Bernd Schmutz
Timothy Smith
Eleanor Suess
Jonathan Taylor

Eight tutors involved in the Kingston University research project that inspired this book came together with architecture critic Phineas Harper to discuss the significance of the public house to the city, and to architectural design.

Phineas Harper The facade of the Jerusalem Tavern in Clerkenwell proudly asserts that it dates from 1720. The building was constructed in the 18th century, but it only became a pub in 1996 when John Murphy (a branding consultant noted for christening the Hobnob biscuit) took it over for his new brewery, St Peter's. The Jerusalem flies in the face of those who argue a truly great pub requires historic authenticity. The pub is a modern confection and yet it's outstanding; cosy, intimate, rich with texture and detail. It is in no way impoverished by its surprisingly recent history even though so many similar attempts to create new pubs have left London with some deeply unsatisfying spaces that feel hammy or sterile. The eight of you have studied hundreds of pubs across the capital. What did the Jerusalem get right?

Timothy Smith Starting with architectural geekery, I think that what the Jerusalem gets right is a balance between artifice and anthropometric dimensions. It's small.

When busy it gets tight at the bar but there are nooks where you can comfortably sit in corners and glazed screens that compartmentalise the place.

Jonathan Taylor It is a bit too small, but like the Red Lion on Jermyn Street you always find a place where you can nestle. The Red Lion's slightly baroque bar is curved so, in a real crush, you can form a little group in the crook. It's only probably eight inches of depth but it's just enough. Some modern pubs are just too big. Think of the barn-like 1998 Sergison Bates pub in Warsall – there's no compression. You don't get that intensity which a really good pub gives you.

Eleanor Suess Pubs have temporal scale as well as spatial scale. Their space is activated by people. We've been talking about the design of pubs from the point of view of our own bodies inhabiting the space, but actually the bodies of other people; kids being loud, a crowd changing the acoustics, people playing pool – without that animation, it's a very different sort of space. The other thing is the spatial layering that goes on. In many pubs, we can see through from one space to another, sometimes through to another again. Sometimes that space is the bar. Sometimes it's the space of the pub reflected back at us through the mirror above the bar. Many great pubs are layered spaces.

Daniel Rosbottom Layering is also about time. The Jerusalem has managed to make something that feels old and layered but they didn't start from scratch. I think the capacity of a pub to change and take on different ideas is crucial.

TS There are pubs like the Cittie of Yorke (p70) on Chancery Lane with big Victorian rooms which are not small or cosy like the Jerusalem. They're part of a bigger city life and can accommodate an awful lot of people while still having a place that you can make comfortable.

Bernd Schmutz Although the Jerusalem is more sober than older historic pubs, it has quite a rich surface compared to a German Beer Hall. The architecture disappears behind the interior. There's an intensity – a sort of panoramic interior landscape. There's no hierarchy between artefacts and objects, taps and tiles – it all becomes one thing.

DR I'd also say there is a sense of ambiguity between publicness and domesticity. Often

in big pubs, you're looking for the threshold between being part of the hubbub of noise, and finding a moment where you can actually hear a conversation. The Jerusalem does the opposite trick. It's quite a small room but because it's quite a hard room, it has a big acoustic. It's not like a living room, it has a sense of publicness even though you put 12 people in it and it's full. There's the ambiguity: the size of a living room but the sensory 'publicness' that evokes another scale of space. Successful pubs often seem to embody many scales within themselves.

PH Is there a kind of recipe of architectural moves that roughly add up to a great London pub? Can we distil the qualities of London's pub character into architecture?

David Knight There is a certain intensity of use and people that comes from a city like London which has led to our pubs tending to be quite particular. The Wenlock Arms (p123) in Hoxton, for example, combined its landlords' love of jazz music and real ale to create a very specific, very generous offer to those communities.

TS I wonder if there's something particular about London's pubs in that there is a grand interior architecture to them – an elaborateness. The boozy drunkenness, the business meeting, the first date, the bloke sitting on his own at the bar with a book and a pipe – all surrounded by an architecture that people mostly can't have at home. A public house is not the same as just a house made public, but it's more like the sort of house most of us can't afford made public.

DK Snob screens and similar devices were used to divide people by class and by price, almost by profession and public standing,

and to divide consumer from staff. The way that was resolved architecturally was a single grand interior (in a slightly debased kind of Classical language) and then the dividing screens would be secondary elements with a clear gap between the overall language of the interior and the subdivision of it. I'm not saying that subdivision of customers by class was good, but the pub usually managed an elaborate game of balance between being together and being separate. Pubs obviously represented the divisions in society at particular moments in time but, through that language of an overall interior, transcended them.

BS I find the ceiling important. The pub ceiling holds everything together.

DK In a pub you're all under the same roof.

TS I worked in a pub that had three separate bars: the Essex Bar, the Victoria Bar, and the Public Bar. The Public Bar had vinyl floor, televisions and dart boards. The Victoria Bar had thick carpet and a cosy fire. And the Essex Bar had fruit machines and kids. I would see the same regulars occupying different bars on different nights of the week. They would bring their wife to the Victoria Bar and their football mates to the Public Bar. There was something quite nice about three different places in one pub.

BS From a continental perspective, British pubs have a certain tolerance to different patterns of use. Compared to a Viennese Coffee House where there's a much more formal choreography, pubs can be used during the day, and at night, they work when they're empty and when they're full. There's a looseness in how they're furnished, in whether people sit or stand. This looseness and tolerance are quite particular qualities.

DR We've discussed divisions and nooks and things that happen in the plan of the pub. But the section is also really interesting. You get screens. You get the bar. You get architecture that seems to engage with you when you sit or when you stand. Two horizons exist inside pubs; one at a standing eye-level and another at sitting eye level. They set up two very different experiences within one very small space.

Cristina Monteiro I feel that the bar is quite a theatrical space, particularly island bars such as in the Wenlock Arms. Going to the bar is like stepping into another world. You get to hear lots of different stories. It's a space where you get transported into other lives and narratives. It's also a space where someone like me now waits for quite a while, and has time to be absorbed by its scenography, the age of the bottles that haven't been washed for 30 years – the patina, the life and the layers of benign neglect of that establishment become really evident when waiting at the bar.

DK The quality of the Wenlock Arms was sealed on my first visit there. I ordered a pint and a sausage sandwich and sat down at one of the tables. The barmaid, who was also an incredible jazz pianist, stood behind the bar marshalling the entire community into a discussion. I had never once been included in that kind of complexity of conversation in a pub before. The Wenlock has a huge island bar that dominates the room, then there's a single row of booth tables around the perimeter. So when you're in that pub, you can be part of a communal conversation at all times.

DR There are different species of pub. If you take a pub, like the Seven Stars (p31) on Carey Street, architecturally it's only a bar, the space in front of the bar, and then the space of the pavement – three very narrow stripes of space stretched out along the length of the street. It is very different from something like the Princess Louise, where you go deep into the plan. Different typologies of pub elicit different relations between the people who are using them. I'm not someone who generally ends up talking to lots of people I don't know in pubs, but actually, if you go into the Seven Stars, you kind of automatically end up as part of the collective conversation. To understand pubs we have to understand how they respond to different audiences. There are pubs within the legal district around Chancery Lane that are specifically designed to allow people to have private conversations, and then there are other pubs which are to do with large numbers of people moving through.

PH Many pubs are also houses. With the Seven Stars for example there are private rooms where the proprietor lives. There's often an entire domestic realm attached to these places that we don't see along with ambiguous multifunctional rooms that are more private than the pub but more public than a domestic space. How do all these private and semi-private spaces fit into pub genealogy?

DK They're absolutely fundamental! We were part of a group trying to protect a pub in North London. One of the issues that emerged was the role of the upstairs function room. It was a vitally important part of its community as a room that was available for use by a diversity of people, but it was also literally home to people who were homeless and

Left: 'The Bar takes over the House', *Inside the Pub*, p64–65

Previous: Interior of the Jerusalem Tavern, Anne Clements

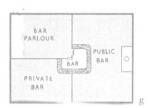

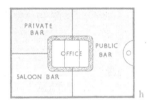

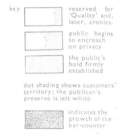

were put up there while they found their feet again. We found ourselves arguing with the planners and a whole range of people in the built environment industry that the pub was not a ground-level use class, it was a complex organism in plan and section that delivered social value in a multiplicity of different ways. You can't just reduce pubs to a story of active frontage and ground floor uses. The fact that the landlord can shut up for the night, and go upstairs to bed in some pubs is fundamental to why it's a good place to go.

JT I think the pub is a complex balance of edifice and institution. The Fitzroy Tavern (p67) on Charlotte Street always had a slightly 1960s interior with vibrant carpet and a gently rowdy atmosphere. It's now been completely refurbished but the atmosphere is almost exactly the same because the crowd is the same. I think the institutional aspect of the pub, which transcends any particular fit-out, is not to be discounted.

CM The Fitzroy Tavern is a dear place to me, but I find the refurbishment that they did really difficult. It might have looked a little scruffy before but the feeling of the place now is a little over-polished. There should be a rule that you can do anything to a pub so long as you don't gloss varnish it or have white lights above a particular lux level! Ensuring that furnishings are not removed or that layering, patina and character that comes with age and use.

DR Perhaps the genealogy of great pubs depends on differences, accretions over

133

time. We haven't touched on the issue of the chain pub. Chain fit-outs are always the same thing shoehorned into different spaces – a predetermined experience.

DK But time can undo that sometimes. I've known pubs that were spoiled by an insensitive or corporate refit and then gradually public use made them feel themselves again. In a pub we used to love there was a regular who was a light bulb salesman. He convinced the landlord to invest in energy-saving light bulbs and when we went in one night the whole place was floodlit like a football stadium. We were collectively outraged that the atmosphere had been destroyed so every time someone stood up to go to the toilet, locals would walk past a light fitting and slightly loosen the bulb so it started to burn out. Gradually we waged a campaign against the new bulbs in an effort to get back the atmosphere. That's obviously a slightly silly story. But it alludes to a larger condition which is the capacity of use over time to steady the atmosphere of a place in the face of an insensitive refit or the commercialisation of an interior.

PH I want to ask about architectural style. Neoclassical flourishes pepper the pubs of London and this book. There's hardly a London pub I can think of without a moulded cornice somewhere. Simultaneously it's really hard to imagine a Parametric pub, or a Deconstructivist pub feeling remotely satisfying. Why are there seemingly few successful Modernist pubs? In what style should contemporary architects approach pub design?

TS To design a great pub, you need to love pubs enough and be observant enough. I think we probably agree that there aren't

many good Modern examples, but there are some! In Poplar there is the Festival Inn by Frederick Gibberd for example that is quite sensitive to what makes a good pub room and is undeniably, unashamedly Modernist. I wouldn't want to go to a Deconstructivist pub, but then I wouldn't want to look at a Deconstructivist building!

DK There were actually an astonishing number of architects involved in pub design, often working directly for breweries. They are not generally renowned designers but there's a lot of skill, attention, care and, I think crucially, a lot of empathy. You don't have to be a hardened drinker to design a good pub, but I think you have to understand how people inhabit space in a way that might challenge how you as an architect expect them to. You can't abstract a public or rely upon truisms of what good design is. There's no rhetoric, there's just community and publicness.

ES An act of sustained observation is required – looking really carefully. Understanding what the qualities and the character of these spaces are to try and define them. It feels that in drawing a pub or filming a pub something can be learned.

PH If you landed a commission to design a brand-new pub tomorrow, how would you start?

JT My first move might be the idea of uncomfortable comfortableness. A bit of tolerable pressure is something that is key to many good pubs. That eight-inch nook in the Red Lion.

TS There's certainly something about specific dimensions and just how small things can be. Pub architecture can be really small if you understand behaviour and habitation. But it needs a looseness – not being overly precious.

DR Pubs teach you to be critical of the Modernist ideas that publicness means immediacy between inside and outside, transparency, that bigger things are more public – that there is this binary opposition between public and private life. Pubs allow us to understand that true publicness is a much more complex experience. I think pubs reveal the potential richness of what public life and public space can be, which we've lost a sense of to a great degree. Public life can be an intimate thing.

BS Whenever I come to England, I like that although each pub has a particular feel there is a familiarity – I feel I've been there before. Good pubs are unpretentious. They don't try to redesign a new atmosphere every time from scratch. If I were to design a pub today, I would find it important to embrace an idea of complexity and multiplicity. Perhaps that is anti-Modernist, because there isn't a set of rules that lets you design.

CM This is one of the most important lessons that we were trying to convey to our students when we undertook the original research that this book builds from. We wanted them to understand atmosphere by trying to capture it and to understand the complexities and nuances of collective inhabitation and public architecture.

ES It's the combination of being able to be secluded and quite private while also being in a public space. The hints of domesticity while being out of the house.

CM You can feel cosy, but you're part of something bigger.

TS Curtains and carpets, soft furnishings and the sorts of things that are not often thought about by architects. How often do you see a curtain photoshopped into an architect's rendering? You don't! But it's precisely the curtain that will make the most austere of interiors work.

DR Pubs remind us that public life has all sorts of gradations within it. That's a really important thing not only for us as architects, but actually for wider society to understand. During Covid we've been able to go to parks, we've been able to walk around in the streets, but we haven't been able to be in a public interior with others. The necessity of that kind of social engagement inside an intimate public space is something that we're now extremely aware of in a way that perhaps we weren't before the pandemic. Multiplicity is an essential part of the metropolitan condition.

DK Pubs remind us that our agency as designers is just part of a much larger cultural act. With the pubs that we've looked at where ostensibly the most interesting thing is the original act of design, it is generally not actually the most profound story. The design supports or creates something else. It may be the first act or the first chapter but usually you come to understand the true value and the quality of that piece of design through what happens in it later. Obviously you want to try to get it right, but ultimately the pub architect is part of a larger story.

The Foundry*

Hackney, EC2A 3JL

'We invite you to exhibit your work at the
Foundry, just ask at the bar', ran an early
Foundry flyer, 'But first there are some
things you should know: this is not an
artist-run space, it is a pub'. From the late
1990s until forced out in 2010, the Foundry
ran as an artfully chaotic bar and venue
with a relentless energy and commitment
to artistic expression whether fine art,
poetry or music, powered by an aversion to
the vagaries of state arts funding. Sunday
open-mic poetry nights were a highlight,
increasingly dominated by 'the Worm Lady',
who turned up one evening with a book of
poems about the significance of worms
and never really left. Alabama 3, fresh from
providing the title music to *The Sopranos*,
once hosted a particularly spirited fundraiser for a jailed collaborator. A lock-in at
the end of the benefit was enforced so that
all guests could empty their wallets into a
bucket before stumbling out into the night.
The Foundry was one of few places where
organic beer by Pitfield Brewery could be
found at the bar, thanks to the brewery being
(at the time) about a minute's walk away at
their original home on Pitfield Street.

Opposite: Assorted Foundry flyers, 2003–2009

1997

The Royal Oak

Southwark, SE1 4JU

Harvey's Brewery has been making beer
by the river in Lewes, Sussex, since the
18th century, and owns pubs throughout
the county but they didn't open their
first London pub until 1997. The brewery
acquired a small, innocuous street-corner
local on Tabard Street, Borough and placed
it in the care of tenants John Porteous and
Frank Taylor who remained in charge until
retiring together in 2019. Behind its net
curtains the pub fostered relations with
diverse groups, among them the Greater
London Council Real Ale Society (still going
strong 35 years after the GLC itself was
abolished), the Players Theatre music hall
and the London region of the Campaign
for Real Ale who make extensive use of the
pub's upstairs function room. The pub is
also the first stop on the pilgrimage from
London to Canterbury (genuine pilgrims
can get a stamp at the bar), making it a
successor to the original Tabard Inn (1388).

Above: Caxton's illustrated edition of Chaucer's
Canterbury Tales depicting the pilgrims feasting at the
Tabard Inn. Courtesy British Library

THE ART OF LISTENING

SELLOUT

**10 ARTISTS
100 WORKS
£9.99 EACH**

Resonance 104.4fm
THE ART OF LISTENING
EXHIBITION

ITEM	PRICE
FRANCIS UPRITCHARD	9.99
GAVIN TURK	9.99
BILL DRUMMOND	9.99
REBECCA HALE	9.99
TRACEY SANDERS-WOOD	9.99
JASON SYNNOTT	9.99
JO SYZ	9.99
DÆDALUS	9.99
RICHARD NIMAN	9.99
KIRSTY WHITEN	9.99

ALL PROCEEDS TO RESONANCE

25TH MAY 7PM
THE FOUNDRY
84-86 GREAT EASTERN STREET EC2
MAY 25-30 TWTH 5-11 FS 3-11 SUN 2-8

normal

DJ/LIVE SESSION
WED 08.10.03
8.00 - 11.00 PM
THE FOUNDRY

sixteen BELTERS for MAD BOB'S DJ SESH

by NORMAL.

Thankyou FOR NOT Urinating on the Carpet

THT ME UP FIVE

TRACEY MOBERLY
DANNY POCKETS
DUNSTAN BRUCE
JAIME RORY LUCY
MOIRA MINGUELLA'S
MESSAGING SERVICE
4th - 21st May 2006
The Foundry
86 Great Eastern Street
London
EC2 3JL
Old Street Tube Exit 3

tel: 07951608787
em: Text-Me-Up-5@foundry.tv

Preview
Thursday 4th May 2006 6 - 9pm

Opening times:
Tues-Fri 4.30-11pm
Sat 2.30-11pm
Sun 2.30-10.30pm
closed Mondays

1998
The Golden Anchor

Southwark, SE15 2DX

Lana Bewry grew up on the Queens Road
in Peckham and worked weekends at various
pubs in Peckham and Nunhead before
getting hold of the Golden Anchor in 1998.
The pub operates a dance hall and is visited
daily by a devoted crowd of dominoes players.
It throws a serious party each year to
celebrate Jamaican Independence Day.

Previous: Marcus Hessenberg

1999
The Social

Westminster, W1W 7JD

The Social opened in 1999 in the wake of the
'Heavenly Social' club nights previously run
by the Heavenly record label at the Albany
(p146) and elsewhere – nights which among
other things had made the Chemical Brothers
into a global household name. The Social
was designed by architects David Adjaye and
William Russell and has a warm and intense
oak-lined ground floor bar lined with leather-
upholstered booths along one side and a second space downstairs for live music, literary
events and DJ sets. During the pandemic
the Social staged daily evening events with a
stellar line-up of guests curating special play-
lists – all now archived on its website. Hosts
have included Jennifer Lucy Allan (p164), David
Keenan, the Magic Numbers, Jude Rogers, Bob
Stanley (p158) and the Windmill (p125).

2000
William the Fourth

Waltham Forest, E10 6AE

Brodie's, an early forerunner of today's independent craft brewers, was born 'round the back' of the William the Fourth in November 2000 with the making of a beer named Sweet William in tribute to the pub. In 2008 James and Lizzie Brodie, whose father owned the pub, revitalised the brewery's output under the Brodie's name and quickly became one of the most highly-regarded of London brewers, with a range of beers so diverse that even the most seasoned beer tickers got confused. An expansive selection of those beers was of course routinely available (until the pub was sold in 2018) at the bar of the William the Fourth, which is a cavernous, riotously popular and richly-detailed corner pub built in 1896 to the designs of W. G. Shoebridge & Lewis.

2001
The Glass Bar*

Camden, NW1 2EF

The founder of the Glass Bar, former accountant Elaine McKenzie, speaks powerfully of the need to make a space where women could meet without being subject to the behaviours of men. She turned words into actions in 1995 when she took over the lease of a long-vacant stone pavilion in the front forecourt of Euston station and opened it as the women-only Glass Bar, running on a membership basis of £1 a day. An informal bar at ground level with a club room upstairs for singles nights, comedy, music and Scrabble tournaments, the Glass Bar was a significant statement in a city where space for women, especially queer women, to socialise is shamefully thin on the ground, making its 2008 closure all the more tragic.

Above: Elaine McKenzie

141

2002

Ye Olde Rose and Crown

Waltham Forest, E17 4SA

Walthamstow Folk Club, a weekly event rooted in the traditional music clubs of the 1960s that spawned the folk revival (Fairport Convention, Steeleye Span, Pentangle) has gone around the houses a few times but is now firmly ensconced in Ye Olde Rose and Crown on Hoe Street. Walthamstow folk legend Martin Carthy played the inaugural gig in the club's new home in 2002. When it's not full of folk devotees the Rose and Crown hosts theatre and panto in its 70-seater theatre. A Freehouse owned jointly by five hands-on landlords, it is a much-loved pub with a focus on beers made by local breweries – which these days means a wide choice as the banks of the nearby Lea river have become a magnet for London craft brewers seeking affordable production space.

2003

The Eagle

Lambeth, SE11 5QY

Formerly known as the Duke of Cambridge and now an established LGBTQ+ bar, the Eagle has since 2004 been the home of the weekly Sunday night event *Horse Meat Disco*, famed for its inclusive, hedonistic 'safe queer space for the disenfranchised disco citizens of London'. The four strong DJ collective behind the event released their first album of original material, *Love and Dancing*, in 2020.

Overleaf: Beppe Calgaro

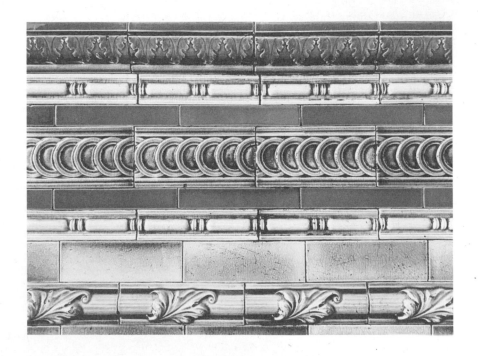

2003
The Prince of Wales

Ealing, UB2 5ED

Desi Pubs combine the qualities of a traditional boozer with a South Indian food menu, and were typically set up in areas with significant Southern Asian communities such as West London and the Midlands. A leader in the London context has, since 2003, been the Prince of Wales on the western fringes of Southall, an area notable as the site of the largest gurdwara in London. Desi Pubs are distinct from grillhouse restaurants, and in this spirit the Prince of Wales runs determinedly as a Freehouse where sport is screened and drinks are served over the bar, resulting in a meaningful coming together of traditions to make a place that feels genuinely multicultural and a powerful statement about community in London.

Above: Tristan Bejawn / Vice

2004
The Masons Arms

Richmond upon Thames, TW11 8PJ

A humble but handsome local on a Teddington backstreet corner packed with a bewildering collection of real ale memorabilia. In fact it's a haven for ale fanatics and if CAMRA were to imagine the perfect local it would closely resemble the Masons. In 2004 the pub initiated the annual Teddington Pram Race, a mile-long sprint with customised hand-pushed buggies or prams, that runs from the pub's front door to the Teddington Fair at Udney Hall Gardens.

The Albany

Westminster, W1W 5QU

Isy Suttie

I'm crammed into the tiny backstage area downstairs at the Albany in Great Portland Street, wondering if anyone's going to actually turn up to watch the show. A small group of us are perching and hovering and pacing into each other, heads in our notebooks, going over our lines aloud, of sketches, bits of stand up, songs – often due to get their first outing that very night – all the while thinking, 'Will this gig even go ahead? Will we be drinking upstairs in half an hour, the adrenaline replaced with relief, wondering why we put ourselves through this night after night?' Then someone peeks around the black curtain and says, 'There's a human being at the bar! The gig's going ahead!' and we bury our heads in our notebooks afresh, our hearts hammering in our throats, knowing there's no going back.

There were some nights at the Albany when I knew we'd have no problem getting an audience. The Book Club began its life in that room, a comedy gig whose bills burst with misfits and geeks and those stand-ups who gloried in the fact they would never play Jongleurs, conceived and compered by Robin Ince. I was flattered and terrified when he asked me to do it, wondering whether to choose my song about a medieval prince who can't yodel, or a silent dance I would perform beside a creepy singing unicorn I'd won at an arcade. We'd walk on to see the audience packed together, all facing the right way, sweaty thighs touching and the room zipping with energy – pure apprehension. Even when someone did something that didn't go down brilliantly, it didn't seem to matter as much as it did in big rooms. Less of a death, and more of a 'I'll try something different next time'.

That kind of experimental, open atmosphere is so much to do with the room. Downstairs at the Albany was perfect for stand up – low ceilings, dark walls, a perfectly functioning but unintrusive bar. (I'll come onto the toilets later). The things those walls had seen! It was virtually a crime to go onstage and do something tried and tested: you felt you should push the envelope in some way. This feeling was due to the architecture, the layout, the comics and, of course, the audience. Not just the size of the audience but how giving they were, which was, in turn, influenced by the architecture, the layout, and, er, who was on stage. (Picture a serpent eating its own tail, guffawing as it does so). The most fun gigs of my life occurred in that room, in the mid-2000s, when I was young enough to remember I was lucky not to be working in a call centre anymore. We were so new to the game that there were no expectations. We could walk on in character

as weirdos who only spoke in lines from *Neighbours* and nobody would question that we were indeed weirdos who only spoke in lines from *Neighbours*.

The toilets were not perfect. They might be now, but they weren't back then. The pungent smell of the drains hit you as you descended the last step into the room, the toilets themselves – the grimy culprits – still many feet away. The smell invaded your senses as you hurtled towards the bar in search of something – anything – to overpower it. If you could forget the smell of those toilets while you were watching the comedy, you knew it was good. Toilets tend to feature heavily in comedians' appraisals of venues. Up The Creek Comedy Club in Greenwich has spacious performers' toilets upstairs, but then they're opposite a gigantic mural of the Last Supper which replaces Jesus' disciples with drunk comedians, so it's a cut above in so many ways. With most pub gigs the performers tend to be awkwardly hunched next to audience members in the queue for the loo, listening to them discussing how they're tired from their job as an estate agent, which comedians they're looking forward to seeing and which they haven't heard of, and how they hate medieval princes and yodelling, unaware you're standing next to them, your pulse racing horrifically,

wondering how quickly you can rewrite your medieval prince song to be about an estate agent in the queue for the toilets who's cheating on their girlfriend with Melanie from accounts.

The fact that the toilets at the Albany had such smelly drains only added to the charm of the venue. Its one supposed flaw merely highlighted its outstanding qualities: with drains that weren't smelly, it would have been completely perfect, and thus intimidating. Its drains gave it humanity. And the toilets at the Albany were as important as the stage itself. It's where we went when we first arrived before they opened the doors, to run things in front of the mirror, our voices echoing off the walls back at us. It's where we did our makeup while running lines or fretting about whether to try that new bit, where we laughed and worried and, sometimes, cried together. And it's where we went at the interval, buzzing, sweaty, with black eyeliners hanging forgotten from our fingers as we debated the fact that we'd 'got away with doing that bit.'

When I started out doing the open mic circuit, there were certain London pub gigs where I'd take my bag onstage with me, lest it get stolen. There were gigs where everyone including the landlord had no idea there was a free comedy night on, and the cries from the regulars as the jukebox got turned off so that the show could begin were louder than any laughter we'd get all night. There were gigs like *Pear Shaped* at the Fitzroy Tavern (p67) which would go ahead with just one audience member, or – as I found out the second time I did it – one audience member and his dog. There were gigs in the function rooms of pubs I'd previously worked at, and as I wove through the tables towards the stage, I'd be hit by the memory of serving lukewarm soup and paninis to

Isy Suttie performing at the Albany in 2007.
© Isabelle Adam

149

German tourists frustrated at my waitressing skills.

One of these was the Red Lion on Great Windmill Street, a pub steeped in history which is now (drum roll…) an All Bar One, where in 1847 Karl Marx and Frederick Engels drafted the *Communist Manifesto*, and where I'd watched Lady Diana's funeral in the kitchen staff's living quarters, drunk on gin. The upstairs room in the Red Lion (I refuse to refer to the pub by its new name, a bit like when one of my female friends gets married) may have worked for Karl Marx but wasn't a great room for a gig: it was square-shaped, with windows that let in too much light, and no natural stage area. I'd love to say that as soon as we skipped onstage and started to weave our magic, such was the hilarity of what we were saying that the room changed into the perfect venue, but that would be profoundly untrue. My unicorn dance was met by faces of confusion and pity, probably from the same German tourists I'd served the soup to in my previous life. Once, inexplicably, Daniel Bedingfield came in before the gig started and all the acts stood in a line like he was the Queen as he wished each one of us good luck.

But any room can be turned into a comedy gig. So many pubs, especially in Soho, have wood-panelled stairs leading up to 'comedy nights'. What's up there? There might be lighting and an experienced compere, or there might be six or so trembling acts with no mic but a modicum of hope, praying for – and at the same time dreading – the arrival of a person or dog so that the gig can go ahead.

We were spoilt with the Albany. The room was for us, not against us. Often I'd double up, doing a damp squib of a pub gig at 8:30pm, then powering through Soho and up Great Portland Street, my guitar straps digging into my shoulders, scribbling my set list onto my hand in biro as I walked, then curving down the stairs at the Albany. I'd hear the audience before I saw them. I'd certainly smell the toilets before I saw them. I'd hear Robin Ince, or Josie Long, or Gary le Strange doing their brilliant craziness to roars of joy and excitement. I'd stand at the bar watching, knowing that after the interval I would try a new song out for the first time, a ballad about a lonely accountant called Martin who slept in bed with a fry up for company, and I'd know that even if it didn't go as brilliantly as I hoped and dreamed it would, and even if while I was doing it the audience remained partially aware of the smell of those bloody drains, I would nevertheless feel, for a fleeting moment, completely and utterly alive.

2009
The Southampton Arms

Camden, NW5 1LE

2010
The Old Orchard

Hillingdon, UB9 6HJ

Cliches like 'authentic', 'old school' and 'proper boozer' abound in reviews of the Southampton Arms. It is cash-only (or was, until defeated by Covid), vinyl-only, eschews booking, with a meat-centric bar menu and a deliberately austere interior which is evocative but noisy. All this was actually created, though, in the late 2000s, making the Southampton an exemplar rebooted Alehouse. Its rules and regulations extend to the beer choice, which is similarly exemplary and limited to independent breweries, with a long row of pumps devoted to independently-made ciders and perries. Live music and a house piano occasionally replace the turntable and virtuoso pianist Holly Roberts – formerly of the Wenlock Arms (p123) – can occasionally be found ensconced.

Overleaf: Andrew Ridley

Originally a sprawling country house dating from the early 20th century, the Old Orchard opened as a pub in 2010. It sits alone in a large landscape overlooking the Colne Valley and the Grand Union Canal. The view is epic and the pub provides extensive terracing and a beer garden to enjoy it from. Thanks to its position on the fringes of Greater London and so close to the Colne, the pub is popular with walkers, boaters, cyclists and bikers.

Quiz
Monday
8.30pm

Live
Piano -
Tuesdays and
Wednesdays
8pm.
+
Sundays 6pm

Please don't
feed our
beautiful
dog Fred.

Thanks and
happy drinking!

2010

The Woodbine Inn

EN9 3QT

Luke Turner

The Woodbine is a bright blue but otherwise superficially nondescript pub situated across the road from an old thatched cattle trough and an Epping Forest glade. Its origins are obscure. A plaque set high up on the wall proclaims that the pub was rebuilt in 1887, nine years after the act of parliament that saved the adjacent ancient woodland for the people of London. Landlord Rob Chapman believes that the Woodbine probably began life as an informal drinking parlour or Alehouse serving beer to drovers taking livestock to market in London. This was exactly the sort of establishment that provoked ire among the patrician moralists of the Corporation of London back down in the City Guildhall. They had used the tax on coal and grain being imported into the capital by ship to purchase the 12-mile-long woodland as 'the people's forest', preserving it forever as a place of recreation and respite for the poor of overcrowded East London. Yet the cockneys didn't obediently do what they'd been told, and visit Epping Forest for edifying self-improvement. Instead, they brought their thirsty sociability with them. In one 19th century speech Chairman of the Epping Forest committee, James Salmon, said he 'hoped that the Conservators would put a stop to the drinking on the Forest and the rolling of barrels of beer on to it, and the turning of it into a wretched place for drink and debauchery.' After the speech, he presented each of his married keepers –

the forest's special constabulary – with a sober pound of tea.

The keepers frequently reported drinking establishments bending licensing rules, or being suspected as the haunt of prostitutes. On 12 June 1875, a frothing editorial in the *East London Observer* complained of Londoners that 'they enjoy the scenery less than the mild ale or other strong potions available in the local inns, while some of them make night and day hideous in their going and returning'. This has continued into more recent times – Chapman himself says that 'the Woodbine has had a chequered past. Before we had it, it was a *Star Wars* bar – a really rough place'.

The Woodbine feels like an outpost of old London, the London that moved east up the railways and trunk roads from Stepney, Leyton, Poplar, Bethnal Green and Bow to find a better life in the new housing estates and New Towns of Essex. A flag of the three-cutlassed coat of arms, historic symbol of the county, might fly on the pole outside the pub, but really this place belongs to the capital, or the East End – that part of London that gave Essex its life and soul. It sits just inside the M25, as if caught by the motorway's lasso, the traffic roaring past a few metres away.

Transport and the expansion of London has always had a profound influence on this part of Essex, pushing and pulling at the boundary between the urban and the rural.

Epping Forest, a woodland owned by the financial heart of the Capital, is no exception to this blurred dichotomy. Indeed, this is what makes it such a strange, radical and special topography, a supposedly wild place that is anything but. Epping Forest's trees are shaped by centuries of coppicing and pollarding for use as building material and especially fuel for London's voracious bread ovens, factories and breweries. Just as Epping Forest defies preconceived notions of nature, so the Woodbine doesn't have the trappings of a traditional country pub: a fire crackling in a grate, twee, wall-mounted rural paraphernalia, faded photographs of old codgers at the bar.

Instead, the Woodbine reminds me of the sorts of pubs I drank in when I first moved to East London 20-odd years ago – brightly-lit but unshowy. These places are a dying breed now, and Chapman laments the end of Brodie's Brewery in the William the Fourth (p141), down by the Baker's Arms, E10: 'He was a great inspiration, that was my treat pub. I used to go down and book a room above it, sit there on a Friday night and try as many beers as they had on', he says. 'What with it being in Leyton I never understood how it wasn't full of all the local alchies – all these high-volume ales and weird and wonderful drinks for £2.75, you could get out of your nut for a tenner, absolutely floored for a day. You had to put a gas mask on to go to the toilet, but it was a great London pub, wasn't it?'

The Woodbine thankfully has better bogs, but no less of a devotion to quality booze, and that London pub spirit. This comes from the entrepreneurial attitude of the landlord, who describes himself as an 'accidental publican'. Chapman is a local boy who grew up in Epping. Moving down the Central Line to the East End, he was heavily involved in the acid house scene, DJing warehouse raves in the late 1980s before graduating to clubs like Ministry of Sound and Turnmills, as well as working in pirate radio. After a spell 'having the life of Riley' running a nightclub in China, he returned to the UK and found work collecting building site waste on the Essex-London borders. Frustrated that he couldn't get a decent bite to eat after a shift, he set up a burger van, not doing anything fancy but using produce from the area. He'd park up and sell burgers outside the Woodbine, but the council tried to do him for illegal street trading. Handily, Punch Taverns' financial troubles meant they put the pub up for sale, and by buying it, Rob legitimised his burger business. He had no intention of actually running the pub, but the previous landlord 'ran the place into the ground' and a manager 'robbed us blind', so circumstances forced him to take a more hands-on approach.

The pub is a reaction to the monotony and limitations of the big pubcos that seek to dominate London. 'You could have been decorating, covered head to toe in paint, and can come in and have a decent drink and food without feeling out of place' says Rob. The philosophy of a pub where all feel welcome connects to his old line of work in the warehouse raves and nightclubs of East London: 'I'd never play one new record without playing two that they'd know afterwards, because most of the public don't love music to the degree that they're prepared to dance to something that they don't know – they feel awkward'.

About a quarter of the pub's clientele are locals, the rest are drawn from Essex, East London and further afield, lured by the reputation for ale and the fearsome arsenal of ciders – a cider aficionado pal proclaimed it one of the best selections he'd ever drunk outside of the West Country. Just as they don't turn their enthusiasm for good beer and cider into some twee evocation of 'olde England', so the Woodbine does food right, and while they buy their meat from the same suppliers as Michelin-starred restaurants, it's all served without pretension. What more evidence do you need than the fact they give you Yorkshire puddings with everything, not just beef? I miss their old Sunday roast menu, with its odd numerical codes by each item – I never quite worked out whether it was to indicate how many carrots, parsnips and so on you could expect to get on the plate. Too many pints of Brewer's Gold or Captain Bob had generally been sunk before it was time to count the peas.

It's in this slightly mizzled state that the Woodbine really comes into its own. A few in, you might find Dennis Stratton (once of Iron Maiden) and Dave Edwards (ex-Manfred Mann) setting up for one of their regular gigs in the main pub room. It's on early evenings like that, stumbling from table to bar to loo, that I love to sink into Woodbine forest time, looking out over the road at the darkening treetops, the glade opposite sometimes haunted by cautious deer, their eyes glowing in the lights of the traffic. There's the prospect of a taxi back to Chingford Station, or the number 66 bus wheezing its way up the hill to Loughton, but neither are ever as appealing as, half-cut, plunging back into the Epping Forest gloaming, boozed and happy and shouting, sliding your way back into the city which, despite the shadowy darkness among the trees, you never really left.

Cutting Wood in Epping Forest, according to Ancient Custom, at Midnight, Illustration for *the Illustrated London News,* November 1859

c. 2010

The Betsey Trotwood

Islington, EC1R 3BL

Bob Stanley

London pubs and popular music go together like a horse and carriage, although at the moment it feels worryingly like the horse has bolted. Whether you're talking about the Manic Street Preachers' first London show upstairs at the Horse and Groom on Great Portland Street or Marie Lloyd making her debut at the Eagle just off City Road, there's a tradition that goes back the best part of 200 years and which, right now, feels under threat. Of course you can still hear music in pubs if you look hard enough, but the days of a *Time Out* listing with a dozen different pub shows every night are long gone.

You can blame the pressure of development if you like, the same justification accounted for the loss of pleasure gardens adjacent to pubs – Ranelagh and Vauxhall being the best known – which were redeveloped in the mid-19th century when land values trumped outdoor entertainment. At that time pubs had no license to present plays (Shakespeare, incredibly, could only be performed by royal decree, keeping him out of the reach of the working classes) so they had to disguise any dramatic entertainment within variety performances. The result was the wild blend of comedy acts, jugglers, menageries and singers that made up 'music hall'. Often these halls, built to accommodate this new mix of performing arts,

became so popular that they completely took over the pub, which could be rebuilt to cater to larger, seated crowds. The Eagle, just off City Road, is still there, though the original buildings – including the 'Grecian Saloon' where performances took place – were demolished in 1900.

After the first world war, music hall would be replaced by jazz, swing, and the less coarse and booze-free 'variety theatres'. Established pubs became simple boozers again as the 1920s dance boom led to *palais de dance* being constructed around the country, modelled on the first at Hammersmith. These venues were still in use when the Beatles spearheaded the beat group boom of the mid-1960s. By the turn of the 1970s things had splintered: universities and concert halls hosted hairier rock bands, cabaret clubs like Batley Variety Club would put on anyone pop, from the Bee Gees to Roy Orbison, and the old dance hall circuit gradually changed into discotheques or bingo halls.

Little ground was left for upstart new acts, and the lack of good, accessible music helped the pub rock scene to take off in the mid-1970s. Musically, it was a mixed bag of country rock and R&B, and the only group to cast a long shadow were Canvey Island's Dr. Feelgood. Nonetheless, the scene opened up a network of pubs around London which had function rooms upstairs, basement bars or, occasionally, surviving Victorian music halls still attached to them. The pub would once again become central to British pop.

The very first pub rock venue was the now-demolished Tally Ho on Fortess Road in Kentish Town, which a band called Eggs Over Easy made their home. More significant were the Hope and Anchor (p114) on Upper Street, Islington and the Nashville Rooms at 171 North End Road, West Kensington. Both of these became early punk venues. The Nashville Rooms, which could hold 600 people, put on the Stranglers in 1975, the Sex Pistols in 1976 (supporting Joe Strummer's 101ers that April) and, in punk's peak year of 1977, Siouxsie and the Banshees, X-Ray Spex, Adam and the Ants, Wire, Kevin Rowland's band the Killjoys, the Jam, Ultravox, Squeeze, XTC, Elvis Costello, Billy Idol's Generation X and the Police.

These venues were training grounds as well as flash points. The Sex Pistols caused instant notoriety, but for the likes of Squeeze, the Police or Adam and the Ants, commercial success was a couple of years away from their shows at the Nashville Rooms. Without the pub circuit, they would have struggled to find anywhere that would take a risk and let them gain experience.

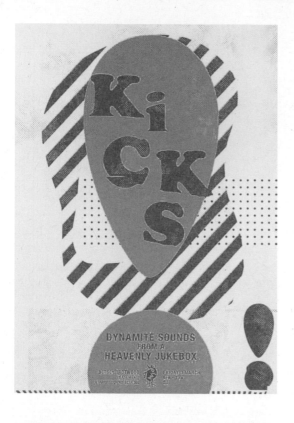

The indie scene that grew out of a dissatisfaction with the gloss of high-1980s pop expanded the pub circuit further. The first album released on Alan McGee's Creation label was *Alive in the Living Room* in 1984. McGee had started The Living Room upstairs at the Adams Arms (which had been a folk club called Dingles in the mid-1970s) on Conway Street, near the foot of the Post Office Tower, with a standard lamp for lighting, a slide show, and no stage to speak of. Still, future stars of the indie scene including the TV Personalities, the Pastels and the Loft played there. The room is largely unchanged, with its bar and fireplace intact, but is now a dining area. Having changed its name to the Lore Of The Land, it is currently run by Guy Ritchie's Fatboy Pub Company, and seems unlikely to be hosting the Pastels any time soon.

Camden Town and Kentish Town would become the heart of London's independent scene in the 1980s. There was the back room at the Dublin Castle on Parkway, where Madness appeared regularly in the early days; the Bull and Gate on Highgate Road in Kentish Town, a proper music hall attached to an attractive boozer; and another venue the Manic Street Preachers played early on. The St John's Tavern in Archway also had a music hall that had morphed into a 'Wild West Room' by the time it became a regular venue for Billy Childish's Headcoats and their fellow garage-punk Medway acts in the 1990s. These last two hold-outs eventually succumbed to gentrification, and both music halls are now dining areas.

The Falcon and the Black Horse were both in something of a no man's land between Camden Town and Kentish Town, classic boozers which happened to have largely unused spaces ready for a pop fan stroke promoter to turn into new venues. Both became clubs run by Jeff Barrett who was the press officer for record labels Creation and Factory before setting up Heavenly Records in 1990. The Black Horse had just a metal spiral staircase leading to its stageless function room, but it did have a stuffed heron on a mantelpiece just behind where Pulp, Carter The Unstoppable Sex Machine, The House of Love and Happy Mondays played. The Falcon, just around the corner, was notorious for its foul-mouthed, David Crosby-lookalike landlord. The venue was down a narrow corridor in a room that may have once been stables but by the late 1980s was a black box that could hold maybe a couple of hundred people. In the summer, that back room was hot, sticky and smoky. The smoking ban would be one of the reasons for gig-friendly function rooms being repurposed. Another was noise pollution. A few years ago, the landlord of the Adams Arms was mourning the fact he couldn't recreate The Living Room even if he wanted to, as the area around Conway Street had become more residential (and with more curtain-twitching middle-class residents) than it was in the 1980s.

By the turn of the 1990s, the Water Rats – once known as the Pindar of Wakefield, and Karl Marx's local – on Kings Cross Road had become the pub to play for groups on the way up. Oasis played their first headline London show there in 1993, which added to its fame. Record labels began seeing the Water Rats as a good venue for 'secret' shows – ones to get journalists excited, and the pub took more money from its back room than it did from the bar. Before too long, the bar became more of a holding area for people waiting to get into the gig, its regular pub accoutrements mostly stripped out. This is a fate that has met many pubs that previously balanced music and the wider responsibilities of a public house: an unhappy compromise – not really a proper club and not really a pub either.

Even if they have managed to survive pressure from the smoking ban, tax increases, rising property values, gentrification and coronavirus, London's pubs will still need to turn a profit, so is there any chance of them becoming homes to temporary music venues again? The history is so strong, you would hope the odd landlord might be philanthropically minded enough to keep music in their boozer. I can think of a blueprint. For the last few years, the best pub in London for inexpensive live music (and good beer) has been the Betsey Trotwood on Farringdon Road in Clerkenwell. There's a ground floor bar, an atmospheric basement bar, and a first-floor function room, meaning that multiple performances can take place at once while the main bar continues as normal.

I had my 50th birthday party at the Betsey; I took my lad, Len, to his first gig there (Birdie, in case you wondered); I've nattered to Suggs in the bar; and I've got to play some obscure Del Shannon and Gene Pitney singles to a dozen or so interested punters, while people downstairs were enjoying an uninterrupted pint. So it *is* possible. You just have to hope that the Community Ownership Fund and other initiatives designed to save pubs can also preserve their status as a hive for British popular music, and that pubs like the Betsey keep on demonstrating that a music pub is a viable and important thing.

Previous: *Vauxhall Pleasure Garden*, 1809, etching by Thomas Rowlandson. Courtesy Metropolitan Museum

Left: Gig flyers from the Betsey Trotwood

2011

The Anchor and Hope

Hackney, E5 9HG

Jennifer Lucy Allan

It is August 2011 and there is rioting in the streets of Hackney. I have friends visiting so instead of staring at the TV, I walk with them down the River Lea to my local, the Anchor and Hope. There's a few people in and the big telly is locked to BBC News. The helicopter on screen is close enough that we can hear the blades both through the TV speakers and overhead. People are coming and going. Glasses clink against the London Pride pumps as they're filled. Two regulars start yelling – one bemoans the violence and calls for the rioters to be locked up, the other says the authorities have been using stop and search on local teenagers too prodigiously. My friends and I have our phones out, and someone at the bar shouts over to ask what we're seeing on Twitter.

The dominant sounds of the pub that night were verbal exchanges of information about what was happening outside. It was an exceptional event, one where the usual pub soundscape was usurped by a barrage of information, and I noticed the contrast. Afterwards I began paying more attention to those ambient sounds, to what I knew about a pub from how it sounded, on nights I wasn't being updated on a crisis.

If you walk into a pub with your eyes closed, the sounds you can hear will tell you what sort of establishment you're in.

The clink of glass on metal means real ale. A foamy hiss from the pumps means plastic sprinklers on the spouts and you're up north; a slosh means no sprinklers and no head on your beer – you're down south. Guinness is notably a silent pour, unless the pub has the sort of deathly silence that denotes a truly unwelcoming place, and the thin exhale can be heard. The steam wand of a coffee machine probably means daytime and seems, anecdotally at least, to be found in bars also serving craft beer.

Is there a jukebox? A DJ? Is the music piped in from a Spotify playlist behind the bar or have you stumbled into karaoke at the Dolphin in Hackney, or perhaps club singers at the Palm Tree in Mile End (p93)? Wetherspoons have no music, because it saves money on the PRS license (bands are paid a fraction of a penny through the Performing Rights Society every time a song of theirs is played in a pub). Fruit machines were allowed after 1960, and if you listen carefully to their trilling you can tell the difference between a win or a lose. If there are sports on the big screen you might even be able to tell what time of year it is, and the languages spoken or accents indicate what local community you're in.

At the heart of this is the last orders bell – the ruler of this soundscape, silent until the final half hour of the night. The bell conveys crucial information. It is rung once for last orders at the bar, and again to say sales have stopped. Those familiar with pubs take the meanings of its rings for granted, but websites aimed at international students and travellers to the UK have paragraphs of text demystifying these patterns for new arrivals.

The last orders bell is the most distinctive and meaningful sound in a pub (and the most dreaded) but it's unclear where its use originates. The bell is connected to licensing laws which dictate opening hours and drinking-up time. A ten-minute drinking up time was added in 1961, later extended to 20 minutes by an act of parliament in 1988. My parents, born in the late 1950s, remember bells at the pubs of their youth, but in a 1970 British Pathé film that voxpops a Boozer when Britain was reviewing its drinking laws, there is no bell, the landlord just calls out 'last orders' to the drinkers.

It is possible that the last orders bell has only been used for a generation or two. There are no newspaper puns mentioning bells prior to the 1980s, save for references to the stock market. It may have come over from the financial or maritime industries – closing bells ring to sound the end of trading at stock exchanges, and at Lloyd's of London a bell was rung twice to mark the arrival of a ship, and once to signal a ship had been lost. Given that both institutions are found in London, is it possible that use of a bell to mark last orders began in the capital?

The bell is little mentioned in Inn-keeping literature, despite its power over the pub and its punters. In his 1939 book *The Local* Maurice Gorham lists the landlord's sequence of shouted calls going out as the pub closes, but no bell: 'Last orders gentlemen please!' 'Time gentlemen please' 'Drink up gentlemen please' 'past time gentlemen please'. A last orders bell is not mentioned in *The English Pub* by Michael Jackson, *The English Pub* by Andy Whipple, or *The Death Of The English Pub* by Christopher Hutt. *The Traditional English Pub: A Way of Drinking* by Ben Davis discusses space, surfaces, objects and lighting, but never the last orders bell (although he does bemoan pubs with poor acoustics where one is bombarded by ever-increasing volume of voices trying to shout over one another).

Why is this? Are we all cognitively blocking out the last orders bell, as that which tolls the death knell on our fun? Its purpose is what makes the last orders bell important. It is what could be considered a 'soundmark' – for the acoustic community of pub drinkers. The soundmark was first defined by Canadian composer Raymond Murray Schafer in 1977, as 'a community sound which is unique or possesses qualities which make it specially regarded or noticed by the people in that community'. He was thinking about the city-wide sounds in Vancouver such as the enormous horns atop the Pan Pacific Hotel which sound the first four notes of *O Canada* every day at noon, and the 19th century Woolwich-made cannon sited in Stanley Park which fires each evening at nine o'clock, but also 'church bells, foghorns, railroad signals, factory whistles, and fire sirens.'

Bells have a role in all parts of life – churches ring bells for births, deaths, marriages, clock bells count out time, the death knell. In medieval Europe and Tudor England, a curfew was an hour at which a bell was rung to signal that all fires must be covered or put out, in order to prevent domestic fires that spread. The root of the word, 'curfew' is from the French '*couvre-feu*', meaning 'cover the fire'. Plenty of bells are classed as soundmarks, Big Ben's bongs being the obvious London example, but what about the last orders bell?

Its absence in otherwise rigorous research on public houses, is not surprising. In discussions around heritage and meaning, there is traditionally more attention paid to that which we can touch than ephemeral aspects of a place, such as sound. However, while there are small variations in the way last orders are managed across different pubs the bell has a crucial role as a marker of time, and it serves to highlight how the things that feel familiar about our locals are as much about what is intangible as what isn't.

Should the last orders bell be protected? There are questions over what it means to protect a sound with such a specific function but a generally available means of creation such as a bell, and UNESCO's intangible heritage is not well suited to such cases. Some sounds have been protected outside of their usual function – I have written in the past about the foghorns switched on for tourists, not to alert boats in foggy weather – but to sound a bell outside a pub is not to sound a last orders bell at all, it is just to sound a bell. The bell requires the pub, and the pub requires the drinkers, and the last orders bell is the essential marker of time in this cycle.

A few weeks ago I returned to the Anchor and Hope and sat outside for the first time in a year. Its soundscape is much changed again, as I could not yet sit inside, and the glass was replaced by plastic for everyone except the very-regulars. As pubs begin to open, I know that a return to 'normality' is not just about the way we sit, stand and drink in our pubs, but in the way they sound too – in the bustle of a Friday night pub full of laughing and shouting, in the slosh of ale in pint pots, and even the unwanted ringing of the last orders bell.

Town Hall & Technical Institute, Leyton

2010
The Hope

Sutton, SM5 2PR

Located in a tightly-knit street in the old bit of Carshalton, the Hope was threatened with closure in 2010 until a determined group of locals came together to take on the tenancy, eventually also buying the freehold in 2015. Shares are restricted so that no single individual among the 46 shareholders can dominate the pub's running, which must mean that a clear consensus has been achieved in favour of old-school pubbing and excellent beer with seven hand pumps, seven keg lines and, in a normal year, regular themed beer festivals and theme-evenings focussing on, for example, sours, dark beers or mead. The Hope also hosts *Green Drinks*, a monthly social to discuss environmental issues over a pint.

2012
The Leyton Technical

Waltham Forest, E10 5QN

The Technical inhabits an extraordinary 1890s Italianate civic building originally designed as Leyton Technical College, a pioneer secondary school and evening class institution providing a technical education to its community. The exuberant facade uses stripes of stone and brick, elaborately carved blind niches in the form of a triumphal arch, and elaborate finials. When the college moved on in 1938 (eventually becoming part of the University of East London) the building became Leyton Town Hall and, after 1965, council offices. It now operates as a business centre and its fine ground floor rooms have, since 2012, housed Leyton Technical, which does a good job of making the expansive, lofty civic spaces of the building feel cosy and intimate whilst retaining their character. The pub is packed out on Leyton Orient match days, and hosts both tap takeovers and speed dating.

2012
The Cock Tavern

Hackney, E8 1EJ

Howling Hops Brewery, now brewing out of Hackney Wick, began in the basement of the Cock Tavern on Mare Street in 2012. Since then the Cock has been one of East London's craft beer go-tos, with 24 seperate beer lines and regular tap takeovers by emerging and critically-acclaimed independent breweries. The pub building is an austere but beautifully-crafted Truman house of the 1930s.

2012
The Faltering Fullback

Haringey, N4 3HB

An enduringly popular Irish pub on an otherwise quiet 19th century residential backstreet west of Finsbury Park, with atmospheric rooms and a multi-storey beer garden tucked away to the rear. Sheffield band Slow Club filmed the video for their single *Beginners* in the pub in 2012, which consisted entirely of actor Daniel Radcliffe miming, apparently having spent slightly too long at the bar, but allowing a glimpse of the pub's richness and complexity.

2013
The Chandos Arms

Barnet, NW9 5DS

Emily and Are Kolltveit took on the Chandos in 2013 and five years later won Best Local in the Great British Pub Awards. Both have a background in music; Emily is a former Mediæval Bæbe and Are is a sound engineer and record producer, and the pub is home, also since 2013, to the Chandoz Jazz Club. In 2020 Emily became curate at Saint Mary's Church, Primrose Hill, though the church has a brewery in its basement with beers blessed by the Bishop of Edmonton, so the transition may be quite smooth.

2014

The Joiners Arms

Southwark, SE5 8RS

Lily Waite

The Joiners Arms in Camberwell is not a queer pub. It is a fairly ordinary South London pub, split over two rooms at the bottom of Denmark Hill. To say the Joiners is nondescript may be doing it a disservice, but it is unassuming; it serves pretty much the same fare as countless other pubs and attracts a mix of locals and students. Though it shares a name with the now-closed, legendary gay venue in Shoreditch, the two are very much not the same.

Regardless, the Joiners quickly became my local as a first-year student at Camberwell College of Arts. There can be an unparalleled excitement to be found when leaving home and making your way– in whatever way that is – for the first time; in exploring a new area and, importantly, discovering a new place to drink. Though the Joiners holds some significance for me with regard to that sense of newfound freedom having flown the nest, it's not alone; other pubs around Camberwell Green do much the same: the Old Dispensary; the Tiger; the long-since closed British Queen – a favourite of ours for its alarmingly cheap spirit mixers and pints of John Smiths, and a lovely, if bemused at the sudden arrival of baby-faced art students in her apparently Millwall-themed pub, landlady.

The significance of these pubs for me lies not in their ambience, architecture, or beer offerings. These are the spaces in which I first began to publicly explore my identity: as a young queer, trans woman unsure of quite who I was, or how and where I could find that out, I was presented with relatively few options to do so. While art school is perhaps liberal-minded by definition, the painting studios didn't provide a playground for gender exploration and expression in the same way that pubs or clubs did. In the studio, my identity was loosely preordained by nervous first introductions and my ID card. On a night out in the Joiners, I was free to be anyone.

Perhaps by virtue of their proximity to Camberwell College of Arts (art institutions, of course, are not just havens for queer and trans kids, but any interesting characters or weirdos, too) pubs such as the Joiners and the Old Dispensary simply felt safer and more inclusive than pubs elsewhere. There were no rainbow flags hanging behind the bar, nor were there signs proclaiming them to be safe spaces, but I can't imagine I was the first gender-questioning queer to step over the threshold, and nor would I have been the last. I got the strong impression that a young trans person experimenting with their gender wasn't the weirdest thing the staff had seen that week.

In hindsight, queer pubs might have certainly been a safer venue for taking these tentative, vulnerable first steps. Though few spaces are 'safe' in any sense of the word for young, early-transition trans people and for trans women in particular, the spaces I inhabited were not necessarily unsafe. In some cases, they were even caring and affirming: most accepted me without question, and the slightly abrasive, yet affable, landlord of the Joiners, Ray, called me 'Princess' in a genuinely endearing manner. Queer spaces, be they pubs, clubs, or events, felt like a far-off possibility – bizarrely, the fear of not fitting in prevented me from setting foot in a gay bar. Though I dreamt of frequenting the Black Cap, the Royal Vauxhall Tavern (p181), or G-A-Y, I was too afraid to ask my friends to join me, and of the idyllic spaces I'd imagined proving disappointing.

But I also recognise now that I'm of a generation for whom queer spaces are not essential. To prior generations of queer folk, figuring out one's identity anywhere other than certain settings would often have been unthinkable. To them, queer pubs meant safety and self-expression: freedom to love, and freedom from persecution, prosecution, and harm. To my elders, my visibility may have been considered a luxury, or a sign of greater acceptance of queer and trans people. So why, then, considering the importance of queer pubs, are they closing at what appears to be a disproportionate rate? University College London (UCL) research from 2017 suggests that 57% of London's queer venues had closed down in the preceding decade.

Certainly, the role of queer pubs has changed. That's not to say they're no longer necessary or valued, but they are no longer the only contexts in which LGBTQ+ people can comfortably exist. Broadly speaking, the world in which we live now is more accepting, and even kinder, to queer and trans people. As such, queer spaces don't offer the same existential relief as they once did: it is now possible for LGBTQ+ people to live our lives authentically, not just behind the closed doors of a select few venues. There is a joy to be found in the freedom to exist beyond ostensibly segregated spaces, and this may well be reflected in the dwindling number of queer pubs. It could simply be that they aren't as important today.

The rise of social media has inevitably played its part, too, not least in light of the coronavirus pandemic. Online was where I found my first queer spaces and, in lieu of venturing out and finding real-world community, sites like Tumblr and Twitter were the first places I found anyone like me. Before the proliferation of the internet and social media, queer pubs were some of the only places where a common understanding could be found. Now the internet makes it much easier to find your people. As with finding community, finding love, companionship, or sex is also no longer relegated to select queer spaces. While some like to blame the rise of Grindr and hook-up apps for these closures, in a 2020 *Vice* interview Alim Kheraj, author of *Queer London*, labelled this view as 'short-sighted'. It's 'the forces of gentrification, which are really why these spaces are forced out', argued Kheraj.

As the seemingly-unstoppable tide of gentrification marches on, queer pubs find themselves at particular risk. I remember the closure of the Black Cap in Camden, though from a distance. Despite its assignation as an Asset of Community Value, the pub – a queer venue since the 1960s – was closed in 2015, reportedly for redevelopment. It's a prospect that either threatens many of the country's queer pubs or has already shuttered their doors, with London's overheated property market to blame for the majority of closures. Thankfully, the legendary Royal Vauxhall Tavern was saved from the same fate (and from the same company) that closed the Black Cap, but it remains one of the lucky ones.

Still, there are reasons to be optimistic. Madame Jojo's in Soho reopened as a burlesque and cabaret venue after a period of closure, while the She Bar in Soho appeared in response to the closure of the only other such lesbian bar in London, Candy Bar. The managers of these spaces are often determined and indomitable people – when the George and Dragon on Hackney Road closed in 2015 due to rent hikes, its successor the Queen Adelaide (p180) opened a matter of weeks later, further up the same street. As Kheraj notes, 'Queer London wasn't the bricks and mortar. It was – and is – the people who create and breathe and dance and live, in those spaces and beyond.'

Perhaps, then, the queer pub is similarly not only bricks and mortar. The word 'queer' is as much a verb as it is a noun – to 'queer' is to recontextualise something or view it through a queer lens – and so perhaps we can queer any pub, finding the safety and comfort we might once have found behind closed doors instead in everyday settings. Though more queer pubs and bars may yet close, the LGBTQ+ community's dogged resilience will endure and we will likely see more open, too, pubs with more inclusive and enlightened approaches to who is made to feel welcome. Much in the same way that the pub played a key role in my exploration of my own identity, so too can it play a role in furthering understanding of queerness and gender variance. As the pub evolves, offering greater provision for sober or mindful drinkers, making space for LGBTQ+ people, and increasingly promoting awareness of sexual safety, it has the potential to play a significant supporting role in queer and trans liberation and subsequent societal progression. Though some naturally take the lead while others lag, the pub's doors no longer function solely to confine queerness or to shield against an often hateful and ever-misunderstanding society and, in this sense, their value cannot be overstated; the joy to be found in a space explicitly for you, in which you'll find people very much like you, is something I imagine is familiar to every queer or trans person. Long may that joy continue.

2014

The Glory

Hackney, E2 8AS

Opened in 2014 by drag queens Jonny Woo and John Sizzle, and 'legendary party-starter' Colin Rothbart, the Glory hosts drag shows and LGBTQ+ performance and art events most nights of the week across the two storeys of its tinsel-tastic interior. Though strongly geared towards performance and spectacle, so much so that its crew run external events at *Latitude Festival* and the National Theatre, the ground floor bar remains very much a pub, a place of freedom and exuberance on the Haggerston Riviera.

Below and opposite: Nicolas Chinardet – zefrographica

2015
Upminster Tap Room

Havering, RM14 3DT

London's Micropubs are thriving in the
Outer London boroughs, often occupying
unremarkable retail units on the city's
network of high streets but occasionally
sited in more unusual nooks and crannies
in the suburban city. Upminster Tap Room
is in the latter group, and has achieved great
things from its tiny base (formerly a garden
centre), squeezed between an optician and
a street of semi-detached houses. In the
Micropub spirit, it is unashamedly a place
where the whims of its management (Bob
Knowles and Caroline Sheldon) reign su-
preme, including an entirely justifiable love
of Dark Star Hophead (it's the only regular
beer) and a mandatory £1 donation to charity
for mobile phone use. In 2020 the latter rule
led to a £2,500 donation to a local school.

2015
The African Queen

Hounslow, TW4 5HL

Namechecked in 2018 by *People Just Do
Nothing*'s Chabuddy G, the African Queen
is a half-timbered Desi Pub that serves up
a decent mixed grill as well as providing a
front bar complete with live sports and a
pool table. It takes its name from the 1951
film classic starring Katharine Hepburn and
Humphrey Bogart, much of which was filmed
at Isleworth Studios about a mile away.

The Antwerp Arms

Haringey, N17 8AS

Jonathan Moses

Sometime around 2007, just as the financial crisis was poised to turn the world upside down, the pubs of London began to smash themselves to pieces. Nicotine-stained paper was ripped away, leaving exposed, raw plaster. Industrial style light-fittings replaced the soft, portentous glow of chandeliers. 'Found' furniture, looking suspiciously like it had originated in a nearby skip, swapped out trusted wooden tables and chairs. All the infrastructure which for decades buildings had been designed to conceal – wiring and air ducts, piping and imperfection – was laid bare. The public house began to resemble a public warehouse.

This trend towards ad-hoc 'deconstruction' began as a marker of hipster cool, imported from the US craft beer scene and the post-Soviet Ruin Bars of Central Europe. But it soon filtered through to the mainstream. In 2007, when I began as an undergraduate at UCL, the decor of the nearby Marlborough Arms (owned by the pub giant, Greene King) was all Victoriana panels and grandad burgundy. A decade later, pockmarked plaster was peeling from the walls like the bark of a London plane. By that point, even Debenhams was sporting a *béton brut* makeover.

Such aesthetic feints can tell us something about the uneasy entanglement of politics and culture over the past 15 years. As the certainties of the prevailing economic doctrine unravelled – first in the financial crash, then the austerity policies which followed – the spectre of previous eras of crisis re-emerged. The trend's most crass iteration was the Job Centre in Deptford, opened at the height of the government's austerity programme, and whose 'quirky design features [were] inspired by its function as a place that once served the unemployed'. More successful was the craft beer company, BrewDog, whose 'punk' style was described by architects CM Design as 'Cold War chic meets abandoned factory'. In one branch, CM commissioned special 100mm thick, rough finished concrete for the bar-tops to sit on a platform of reclaimed bricks, with flooring made of polished concrete and Durbar non-slip industrial steel sheeting of the kind 'used widely in factories and as manhole covers'. This style repackaged the relics of industrial decline into an aesthetic of a Neo-Industrial revival, just as the company's 'punk' branding heralded the resurrection of a faded 1970s subculture; albeit divorced from the contexts which once gave it meaning.

The late cultural theorist Mark Fisher once described this tendency through the concept of hauntology: a 'failed mourning' for a half-buried past which 'will not allow us settle for the mediocre satisfactions one can glean in a world governed by capitalist realism'. And so, after decades of commercial architecture striving to present itself as a pristine commodity – like a Jonathan Ive-designed iPad – deconstruction indicated a striving for the certainty of the tangible, raw and real. Glass and steel, effacing the traces of their users and makers, symbolised an evermore speculative, immaterial economy; the rough finish of concrete appeared to bring it crashing back to earth.

This helps makes sense of BrewDog's attempt to make their bars resemble an extension of their brewery, symbolically collapsing the gap between the frontstage of consumption and the backstage of production. Meanwhile, Taprooms run by craft breweries took off across the capital – with drinkers flocking to industrial retail parks to get their pints straight from the tanker. It's easy to be sarcastic: but behind these gimmicks there seems to lie a desire to do away with the alienation that otherwise shadows so much of consumption.

Yet the limits of these gestures are obvious. Rebellious craft brewers began, one by one, to sell themselves off to venture capitalists and the same mega-brewers they claimed to rail against. Entrants to the industry became increasingly rarefied, with corporate backing present from inception. With no coordinates for the future, a culture which took to tearing down the walls found itself without a vision for how they might be rebuilt: a morbid symptom of the old world dying and the new unable to be born. Meanwhile, the spectral economy continued to do its work. The inflation of asset prices meant the capital's pubs became far more valuable as housing or office space than they ever could as a boozer: since 2001, over a quarter of London's pubs have been lost.

Over the same period however, a different kind of ad-hoc pub began to appear, one which appears to offer a way out of capitalism's envelopment of the capital's Alehouses. The idea of the community owned pub first took root in a rural village in Cumbria but has since spread across Britain. In 2015, London opened its first, with the movement gaining momentum nationally.

Community ownership works by a group of locals banding together to form a charitable organisation, such as a Community Benefit Society, which enables shares to be issued to anyone interested in owning a piece of the pub. With enough shares, as well as additional investment from places like the government's Community Ownership Fund, capital can be raised to offer a competitive bid on a pub in danger of being sold for development. Concerned locals can apply for their pubs to be recognised as Assets of Community Value: giving them advance warning and a six-month moratorium before any sale goes through, effectively buying time to launch a ground campaign aimed at saving the pub and gathering the resources required to buy it. The process can be arduous, but you are not alone: organisations like the Plunkett Foundation are on hand to give guidance, and informal support from the Community Pubs Network on Facebook can help with the rest.

That's exactly what one small community in North London did. The Antwerp Arms, a quiet corner pub adjoining the Tottenham cemetery had been serving drinkers since the mid-19th century. Then, in 2013, locals discovered it was slated for closure and conversion into flats. A public meeting was called, a successful fundraising campaign launched, and two years later, the pub became theirs. Since then, the Antwerp has become much more than a drinking venue: running community lunches, friendship-and-conversation events, grow-your-own food workshops and live music nights. As Ashley Grey from the Antwerp Arms Association put it, 'people love to come in and be part of our story. A lot of what happens in communities is quite top-down and everybody here has done it without that… and that's empowering'.

The Antwerp has its own form of ad-hoc improvisation, but nothing about it is contrived. Volunteers drop in and out to help with the kitchen and other charitable projects. Local artists exhibit their work in impromptu galleries along the walls. Old men take part in games of limbo celebrating Jamaican Independence Day. The pub's aesthetics are simple and unshowy: minimising fussy decor to instead draw your attention to the sunlight which fractures through the panelled windows onto the traditional wooden floor. This is a space which is readily adaptable – not to economic maximisation – but differences of need: a cosy bar for a quiet weekday chat one day, a makeshift canteen the next.

Community ownership isn't perfect. Six months isn't much time to pull together a buyout, especially when the prospective buyer is a heterogenous group of people or a poor community, and sellers can still choose to ignore the offer if the community is outbid. Successful examples are currently limited to more Outer London or suburban conditions where land and property values are lower. If the deal goes through, the complexity of running a business can be demanding for volunteers who may lack professional expertise and are reliant on the goodwill of others to make important tasks happen. Likewise, different visions can lead to rancour and conflict: 'You go into it imagining that a community is a wonderful green field where the lion lies down with the lamb,' as one Antwerp instigator I interviewed put it, 'And when you get to the other side of it you realise it's just a load of muppets who want to bury axes in each other's heads: that's the reality of what a community is!'

Nor are Community Pubs immune to some of the more exploitative practices of the hospitality industry at large: in 2018 the Ivy House in Peckham was the scene of a wildcat strike after relations between bar staff and the community management committee broke down over the use of zero-hour contracts and what the workers termed 'the effective dismissal of staff with no notice given.' Collective ownership may remove some of the pressures of pubs operating in a difficult market, but only principled agreement separates the working practices of a Community Pub from more nefarious industry standards. Though at the Ivy House, at least, an agreement was reached and union recognition for workers achieved.

The pub has always been an ambivalent institution, drawing its legitimacy from tradition while simultaneously finding itself at the mercy of the ceaseless novelty of the market. The trend for deconstruction is just one example in a long history of pubs overhauling themselves to fit current fashions.

And yet in so doing, they undermine the very solidity and sense of permanence which makes the pub such a powerful, enduring symbol within British culture. That dynamic accounts for the air of crisis which has surrounded the pub for at least a century – always, it seems, in the process of dying, and yet perpetually being reborn by the desire to harvest its cultural capital. The pub is a kind of architectural fulcrum in which the residual and emergent are forced together and required to make sense of one another, usually with anxious results. Community ownership offers a way to break the cycle: owned in perpetuity with the sole object of guaranteeing its existence, a pub that has transitioned into community hands is unlikely to ever leave them: removed from the market until the next meteor strikes.

2015
The Marksman
Tower Hamlets, E2 7SJ

Fergus Henderson, graduate of the
Architectural Association and one-time
chef of the French House (p102), opened
St. John in a derelict pork-smoking house
in Smithfield in 1994, with Trevor Gulliver
and Jon Spiteri. St. John's renovation of
the smokery has a down-to-earth, pub-
like intimacy in which pints are just as at
home as the house red. 20 years later two
former St. John chefs, Tom Harris and Jon
Rotheram, went further and took over the
Marksman in Hackney, making a truly
exceptional Gastropub, not just because
the food is excellent but also because it
has survived as a place to prop up the bar
with a pint or gather for a few drinks with
friends. This simple combination is rarely
done well, and here it is done extremely
well. Like St. John the emphasis is on
simple dishes made using outstanding
ingredients. Sitting downstairs means you
dine on fine things in the midst of a bustling
local pub, whilst the upstairs dining room –
with bespoke floor of radiating marbled
Marmoleum strips, painterly ceiling and
bulb-like clear glass pendant light fittings
by designer Martino Gamper – is a quieter
and more formal experience.

Above: Jorge Monedero

2015
The Queen Adelaide
Hackney, E2 9ED

Queer pubs and venues have been disproportionately affected by redevelopment and
rent hikes throughout London. One of the
pubs lost in this process, in 2015, was the
George and Dragon after 13 years making
its particular corner of Shoreditch a haven
for inclusive, joyful queer nightlife. Happily
within a few weeks the management had
found a new home in the Queen Adelaide, an
1830s pub further east along the Hackney
Road, and took their vibe and extraordinary
collection of ephemera with them, including a
beloved animatronic horse's head. Celebrated
architectural photographer David Grandorge
(whose shot illustrates the pub overleaf)
can sometimes be found DJing in the Queen
Adelaide's mirror-clad basement bar.

Overleaf: David Grandorge

2015

The Royal Vauxhall Tavern

Lambeth, SE11 5HY

'The RVT' dates back to 1860 and was built on the site of the Vauxhall Gardens, one of the most significant entertainment venues in London from the 17th century through to the mid-19th. The pub was built just as the Gardens closed down, but it would forever be linked with one of London's great pleasure centres. Its significance to London's LGBTQ+ community began in the 1940s, and the traditional bar-segregation of the public house played a surprisingly productive role in building a gay community at the pub. A partitioned-off bar made it easier – in the context of homosexuality being illegal in Britain until 1967 – for gay clientele to communicate with peers. By the 1970s the RVT was an established centre for drag performance, and in the 1990s the *Duckie* began, a weekly night of queer heritage, performance art and honky-tonk compered by Amy Lamé (now London's Night Czar under Mayor Sadiq Khan) which continues today. When a freehold sale threatened its future in 2014, and after a huge campaign effort by the group RVT Future (including a remarkable listing application to Historic England written by Ben Walters), the pub became the UK's first building to be listed in recognition of its importance to LGBTQ+ community history. This was a watershed moment, marking a turning point in the collective valuing of queer space and of how culture and identity are made in a city like London.

Right: Stills from *What's a Girl Like You...* documentary, 1969. Courtesy British Film Institute

The Hare

Orit Gat

For the Saturday 12:30pm football kick-off, I was usually in bed. I would wake up, pick my laptop off the floor by the mattress, watch the first half snuggled in the sheets, then make my morning coffee during half-time. For much of my adult life, I was living in New York, following the football on my laptop in weird hours and alone. It would sound counterintuitive to many football fans, but it made sense to me. Growing up in the Middle East, European football was an occasion. When games were televised, my dad and I would stay up watching them, often well past my bedtime. In my family, sport was watched on-screen, in quiet living rooms, and for a long time I didn't think this was unusual.

When I was trying to decide whether to leave New York and move to London, a friend told me to add the Hare to the London column on my pro/con list. I thought it was a joke and humoured him. I still have that list saved on my computer, and years later, I think, I didn't go there as often as I thought I would, but my friend was right – the Hare made me feel, even though I was somewhere new, like I was a little closer to something I always loved.

By the time I moved to London I had lived in four different countries, but no one becomes an expert migrant. There are numerous specificities to imbibe about a new place and countless situations that remind you just how much of a stranger you are. The Hare, an old-fashioned pub on a main road in East London, became a social space that facilitated some of this knowledge for me. It was where I learned two things at once – how football wasn't a lonely experience, and how to live in this new country. The Hare has huge windows onto Cambridge Heath Road (though the blinds are mostly drawn). On the top of the building is a big sculpture of a hare guarding the main drag out front. The pub stays open until 1am on the weekends and gets a little wild. It has a worn, patterned carpet and a jukebox and lino floor by the bar. There's a pool table at the back, which means you end up having a bit of a chat as you walk past on the way to the toilet, you trying to navigate the narrow space, the players negotiating the distraction. After the smoking ban was passed, a little backyard space was converted into a smoking area where people stand around cramped (getting there also requires side-tracking the pool players). There are circular high-top tables built around the supporting poles in the middle of the space and on the wall is a huge photograph of London at night, the Thames and Tower Bridge centred in its middle.

It's traditional, or some people would call it a 'proper pub', but I wouldn't know what that entails.

There's a television next to the door, but when the football is on, the photo of London is largely covered by a huge screen. Everyone sits on low, round chairs along the windows, their gazes directed at the match. On a good day (usually when Arsenal are playing) it's so full that if you try to get to the bar to buy a round, everyone groans when you pass in front of them, hiding their view for a split second. It's all very masculine and shouty, but also very friendly. It feels like an atmosphere. If this sounds normal, I now know that it can be rare. I've been to pubs where they played the game, only without sound. I've been to places where the football was in the background, or shown in a side room, places where the football was an accoutrement, part of the decor. This is not what's going on here.

When I moved to London, much of my knowledge of the UK was rooted in football. The geography of the country was made up of the names of clubs, which are actually, obviously, the names of towns and cities. I heard some accents in post-match interviews that I began to recognise. With time I would discover something about local culture and politics from the game. There is joy in that process of learning, when things begin to make sense, and a vocabulary becomes clear. But there is conflict between knowing and learning: what locals carry with them as inherent, almost embodied, knowledge is often so new to me that when it comes up I relate to it in a way that some-how exteriorises my foreignness. Like reusing a clichéd reference you just picked up, or a turn of phrase clunkily uttered. The cultural expectation of migrants is that they assimilate – study the language, follow the ways of a society, abide by rules and customs that are never explained, since they were already internalised by natives. It's often an impossible expectation that sets migrants up to fail.

To be new in a place means to be con-sistently alert to any sense of belonging and exclusion. Every interaction carries with-in it the possibility of making you feel like you belong, or like you don't. When someone describes a pub as 'proper', I feel a linger-ing sense of fear that when I order a round at the bar in my heavily-accented English, I will feel unwelcome. This never happened at the Hare. And anyway, I was mainly there for the game. My experience of trying to prove that I belong around football, a terri-tory consecrated by others – mainly men, often European – feels related to these experiences of migration. I've been lucky enough to be an immigrant by choice and mine was an immigration full of possibilities, rather than necessity. I can't trace back the many moments in which I clocked those small characteristics of a place that lead to a sense of knowing it, when I stopped saying the wrong things or figured out how to recognise and navigate social difference or just figured out how late to show up to a dinner party. I make it seem casual but it's always a looming prospect: the expectation of migrants that they would know things coded into a culture, the numerous landmines in not knowing, the very few ways to learn. The pub became, for me, a communal space in which some of this intangible knowledge can be attained.

Here are some of the things I discovered about football: How the 3pm kick-off on a Saturday isn't shown on television (to encourage people to actually go to games). What the little pint glass symbol on the corner of the screen meant (that the pub has paid for a licence to publicly screen the games). The personalities of commentators I've never heard before because I only ever watched football in other countries. The difference between an ale and a lager (though I'm still not sure I've mastered that one). I thought East London looked familiar but there were accents and affiliations, histories and allegiances and they told me a different story of London that was not blindsided by the (new?) posh side of Hackney. Because it came as part of a time and place – the game, the pub – every discovery had a sense of occasion, a narrative to it, a way to connect.

The Hare: an Arsenal supporters' pub (the owner is a fan) in a neighbourhood I didn't live in became a place of translation. A place that, against all odds – as a woman with an accent, a Liverpool fan, a South London transplant – ended up being where I learned my new environment.

I've seen games in Brooklyn bars: I drank Coca-Cola in Williamsburg because it was too early in the morning for a beer and the bar never served coffee. I tried to understand why there was a Tottenham Hotspur supporters' pub in Bed-Stuy. I learned nothing about the US that way, those were the places in which my difference was shared with others: I was a Middle Eastern immigrant, holding onto the love of a game many Americans thought of as snobbish and European. When I immigrated to the UK, after a lifetime of watching football on a screen from afar, I felt like I got a little bit closer. The Hare was a place that, against all odds, I could navigate. Maybe it could have been a different pub, though the Hare feels special to me, but it could not have been another space. It had to be the pub that proves something I intuited before: how football taught me a way to insist on belonging. Watching football at the pub means finding yourself where you never expected to, still finding yourself.

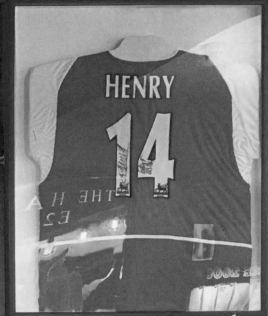

WEMBLEY 1950

HENRY
14

England vs Czech
Republic
Tuesday 22nd June
Tickets still available ...
If you're quick!!

Julian

UEFA
EURO 2020

The Observer

POOL PLAYERS
ONLY!
STANDING

2016
The Lord Napier

Tower Hamlets, E9 5EN

Few pubs have recorded the changes of their local area as vividly as the Lord Napier, which has stood in Hackney Wick since the 1860s. Built as a street corner local at a time when Hackney Wick was rapidly industrialising, the pub initially served the area's thousands of factory workers. After a long period of industrial decline locally, the pub shut in 1995 and then took on a new life as the scene of raves and squat parties as part of Hackney Wick's transformation into a place of creativity and experimentation on the fringes of the Lower Lea Valley. Since the 2010s and the London Olympics Hackney Wick has rapidly gentrified and brick-clad residential blocks now outnumber industrial yards. In 2016 locally-based artist Aida Wilde responded to these changes with a project that covered the building with graffiti commissions, including the now-famous line 'Shithouse to Penthouse'. In 2021 the pub will re-open after a major refurbishment by ZCD Architects and their client Electric Star, who also revitalised the Fellowship in Bellingham (p72).

2017
The Dodo Micropub

Ealing, W7 3TR

The Dodo opened in 2017 in a 19th century terrace in Hanwell. Publican Lucy Do has a stated aim of attracting more women drinkers to beer and building community in her local area. The tiny interior is carefully designed to promote conversation – all tables face into the room – and to make gravity-dispensed beer (no pump) an attractive prospect with a temperature-controlled back room – a cunning idea for pubs operating out of a single-storey unit or otherwise constrained space.

Above: Portrait of Lucy Do

2017
Gidea Park Micropub

Havering, RM2 5HA

Once upon a time, pubs grew from living rooms. Nowadays they grow from accountants' offices, as with the example of the Gidea Park Micropub which sits on a little scrap of high street on the main road into Essex that was once a hamlet called Hare Street. Gidea Park was largely developed in the 1910s–1930s as a model suburb, with many of the most influential architects of the day designing one-off exemplar houses, among them Clough Williams-Ellis, Raymond Unwin & Barry Parker, and Berthold Lubetkin. But the neighbourhood was never masterplanned as a coherent place so remains very much a suburb without a centre. The Micropub is about the size of your average Gidea Park double garage, and is devoted to a regularly-changing beer selection and good conversation sold in an unfussy, stripped-back manner. As is common with micropubs, there's no room for a bar, instead staff retreat to a back room in order to fill your glasses.

2017
The Prince of Peckham

Southwark, SE15 5JA

Landlord Clement Ogbonnaya is aiming for a home from home for all at the Prince of Peckham but there's a definite youthfulness to the pub and it opens late at the weekends. Events happen upstairs in the large music room, in the ground floor bar or in 'The Shrine', a basement bar with a mural celebrating Afrobeat legend and political activist Fela Kuti. The name and the spirit of the Prince of Peckham both originate in 1990s sitcom *Desmond's*, in which a neighbourhood barbershop served as a community centre for an array of black British Guyanese characters – among them Lee 'The Peckham Prince' Stanley.

Below: Portrait of Clement Ogbonnaya

2017
The Bill Murray

Islington, N1 8NQ

The Bill Murray is a reboot of stand-up comedy in the form of a pub, built on the conviction that stand-up should be risky, informal, up-close and accessible, and ideally performed in the back or upstairs room of a pub, one room away from the bar. The Angel Comedy Club had been running in an upstairs room around the corner since 2010 but took on the (quickly renamed) Bill Murray in 2017 following a successful crowdfunding campaign. At its peak it puts on stand-up nightly, running on a 'pay-what-you-can-when-you-leave' basis which not only removes barriers to access but also gives each night the right mix of benevolence and tension that has made the Bill Murray a place where emerging stand-ups can hone their act beyond the open-mic circuit. For all these reasons it has built up a huge amount of goodwill and, faced with the death of stand-up due to Covid, moved rapidly to restage its pandemic survival strategy as a soap opera available only to subscribers, starring club owner Barry Ferns and various 'friends of Bill' including Nina Conti, Adam Buxton and Tim Key. James Acaster's appearance, due to lockdown restrictions, involved an iPad with Acaster's face on it strapped to Ferns' head. The proprietors insist the pub's name is a tribute to William Murray, first Earl of Dysart, though we suspect a certain Ghostbuster may also have been in mind.

2018
The Little Green Dragon

Enfield, N21 2AD

In 2015 the locals of the Green Dragon, a large pub in Winchmore Hill, lost their battle against the pub's closure (including two failed attempts to have the pub listed as an Asset of Community Value) and were forced to watch it become a supermarket. Within two years the Little Green Dragon had opened up almost within sight of the original pub, and within six months had been awarded Greater London Pub of the Year by CAMRA. It's a great and very popular Micropub which squeezes shove ha'penny and table skittles into its tiny interior but also tells a rousing story of a local institution coming back to life.

The Bird and Barrel

Bexley, DA7 6HG

A brewery tap is a pub or taproom close to the brewery itself and operated by the brewery as a front room to its activities. Sometimes in the brewery, sometimes just nearby. In this context we think the Bird and Barrel is unique in London. It's a 'microtap' set up by Bexley Brewery to sell their own beers (plus well-chosen guests) to a local crowd using the format of the Micropub. The Micropub model tends to thrive on a frantic turn around of independently-made beers, so the Bird and Barrel is a bit less adventurous in comparison but the Bexley Brewery, a family concern run by Cliff, Jane and Cameron Murphy, makes reliably good real ale embedded in Kentish hops and in the local communities of Erith, Bexley and Barnehurst. The pub has a micro beer garden out back lined with hops and runs regular beer festivals.

The High Cross

Haringey, N17 9HT

In the early 20th century municipal authorities were building public conveniences on prominent sites throughout London's town centres, often as highly distinctive miniature civic buildings. By the 1980s many of these amenities were closed down and boarded up. With public toilets no longer considered a core service, many have been sold off and others remain closed. The London Borough of Haringey found an alternative beginning with the High Cross in Tottenham. With support from the Greater London Authority the 1920s Mock-Tudor toilet block, built in a language commonly used in that period for loos, changing rooms and pubs, was refurbished and then transformed into a pub by Chris Johnson and Alex Beeston, again supported by the borough. The result is a popular, intimate little pub which has flipped its street corner into a sociable moment on the High Road, and its toilets are open to all when the pub is.

Below: Andy Parsons

Tavern on the Hill

Waltham Forest, E17 5RG

Jaega Wise
Nana Biamah Ofosu

Jaega Wise founded Wild Card Brewery in 2012 in Walthamstow, with William John Harris and Andrew Birkby. Almost a decade later, and with two taprooms open, they have become the new custodians of the Tavern on the Hill and have set about restoring the pub to a central place in its communities – a communal artefact. The pub, which sits atop Higham Hill, Walthamstow, dates back to the 19th century when it was known as the Higham Hill Tavern and, later, as the Warrant Officer. The reimagined pub opened for the first time on 12 April 2021, on the day that pubs across the country were allowed to reopen their beer gardens. Jaega and I settle in the rear garden. It is a sunny spring morning and as our conversation unfolds, the garden comes to life, in time for Friday lunch.

Nana Biamah-Ofosu I want to begin with your career trajectory from chemical engineer to head brewer.

Jaega Wise The trajectory isn't so indirect – all the major breweries have chemical engineers in their teams. Aside from the oil and gas industry, the food industry is a major recruiter for chemical engineering, and I also liked beer – I enjoyed going to

beer festivals, home brewing and learning about beer. Without knowing it at the time, everything I was learning as an engineer was setting me up for this. In my placement year working in water treatment, I learnt all the basics you need to know about water and, as it turns out, that's what makes a good beer – making sure your water is right.

NBO What brought about Wild Card Brewery?

JW I was unfulfilled in my job, so I quit, with no plan. Around the same time, in 2012, Will and Andrew were getting serious about brewing, and I took on the role of organising and production, working with them. We started out cuckoo brewing, which means using another brewer's site, at Brentwood brewery in Essex where we learned a lot from Sophie de Ronde, founder of *International Women's Collaboration Brew Day*.

Our first delivery was tiny; eight casks and about 600 bottles – which we stored in the cupboard under the stairs. We wanted to sell our beers locally and so approached all the nearby pubs. Then came the hard lesson. The majority of pubs in Walthamstow are Tied Houses, which means that they are contracted to a particular brewery or pub

company. The Tavern on the Hill was one of only a few Free Houses that could sell the beer they wanted to sell. When we first came here the door would be closed and you had to knock and wait. They'd take a good look at you and decide whether to let you in. It'd earned a bit of a reputation, having once featured on a TV programme called *The Toughest Pubs in Britain*. We managed to convince the landlord to let us use the basement as storage for deliveries in return for some casks of beer. Within a year, we'd outgrown the basement, but we knew we wanted to stay in Walthamstow. So we moved to Ravenswood Industrial Estate, just around the corner.

NBO You grew up in Nottingham which has a thriving pub culture but, for me, growing up as a first generation Black African in a suburban New Town like Milton Keynes, pubs didn't necessarily feel like welcoming spaces. What does it mean to think of the pub as a community room and what are the implications of creating exclusive spaces?

JW Before our arrival, The Tavern on the Hill had been quiet for a number of years. It had a specific and local clientele, who liked things a certain way. It had a sense of familiarity – it was quite exclusive in some ways. We wanted to create an inclusive space, to redeem the pub's troubled image, but it was also important that we didn't exclude local people. Everyone wants a busy and welcoming local pub, one that feels like the centre of the community. We want to avoid the ills of gentrification that marginalises a pub's local community. Our history within the community, having been in Walthamstow since 2012, helps facilitate these relationships.

NBO Beyond its architecture, interior and atmosphere, it is people that play the defining role, and the way a pub is managed – by a tenant landlord, a landlord with a freehold, management company or brewery. How are perceptions of pub and brewing culture changing to support the creation of more inclusive spaces?

JW Beer and brewing in the UK are very gendered in a way that they aren't in other parts of Europe. Pubs for a long time were not spaces where women were particularly welcome. Historically the pub was essentially divided into two spaces: the bar for the men and the lounge for the women and children. It is very easy to feel comfortable sitting in a cosmopolitan East London pub, but I see a different reality when I travel to other parts of the country.

NBO It is also racialised to some extent.

JW That is interesting to me, reflecting on how my Black African and Caribbean friends embrace pub culture. For me, it is about finding a way in, exploring creative ways of introducing people to new beers. My mum, for example, will tell you she doesn't drink beer and yet there is always

a Guinness in the fridge. Stout is a big thing in the Black community, whether in Africa, the Caribbean or within the diaspora. One of our latest beers is a tropical stout themed around this culture. Similarly, we made a beer with sorrel, a flower related to hibiscus and popular in Jamaica. It was a hit with the older Caribbean women! There is always a way to introduce beer to most communities.

NBO I wonder what opportunities for discovery are sacrificed because of these perceptions.

JW Dea Latis, a group comprising women working in the brewing industry and named after the Celtic goddess of beer and water, have been researching these issues. Their 2019 report, *The Beer Agender*, examined the reasons why women in the UK didn't drink beer. They found out that women were more likely to try a beer when it was introduced by a friend rather than, for instance, going to a beer-tasting.

It is about sensitively engaging with people's preferences. I recently presented a segment about low or no alcohol beers on Radio 4's *The Food Programme* called *Weak, Small, Free*. It centred on the shift in drinking culture, especially among young people, who drink less alcohol than the older generation but were more interested in quality. It is about catering to shifting attitudes and ensuring the pub is an inclusive and welcoming environment.

NBO Early photos of the Tavern on the Hill show it as a Tied House of an East End brewery, Smith, Garrett & Co. At this time breweries played a significant role in the ownership and management of pubs, building up large estates of pubs in the process and obliging their tenants to sell their products to the exclusion of others. Today those large brewery estates have become major property companies and pubs in their care can lack a personal touch. It strikes me that Wild Card, as a young brewer, has a chance to do things differently. What does the distinction between Tied and Free Houses mean for the pub as part of communal infrastructure?

JW When you drink in a place like the Tavern on the Hill, you are supporting local businesses and directly helping the local economy. It is also why I personally choose to run an independent brewery rather than work for a big, commercial producer – surely life is too short and my taste buds too strong for bad beer! The reality is that I can only drink so much in this lifetime, so I'd better make it good.

NBO I want to conclude with the physical presence of the pub, its architecture, interior and atmosphere and what this means in terms of creating a communal place. As a brewer you're unusually involved in the atmosphere of your pub. What makes a public house truly 'public'?

JW One of the first things we did was to change its name from the Warrant Officer to the Tavern on the Hill, partly to draw a line under its troubled history. We have also restored its original features; reinstated the bar, lounge and dining area, revealed the beautiful 19th century timber floor. We removed a later partition wall which had diminished the pub's character. Externally, we made new signage in the spirit of the original, using applied gold leaf.

The atmosphere generated by the architecture, the sense of familiarity and tradition also carries through the way in which you create community through social interactions. As a publican, part of your job is to be a listening ear for the community – it is one of the crucial roles that the pub plays in a local area. The pub as a community room also goes some way towards tackling loneliness. We have regulars that come in at the same time on most days. They don't plan to meet here but they'll come in, sit and socialise together and for a time, they are not alone. The pub offers one of the remaining few opportunities to create spaces of care and community in modern Britain.

2021
The Carlton Tavern

Westminster, NW6 5EU

We'll end with a story of rebirth. In April 2021 pubs across England with beer gardens opened for the first time in months, following an extended period of lockdown in response to the Covid pandemic. The Carlton Tavern, a 1920s pub designed for Charrington by Frank J. Potter, an Arts and Crafts architect who also designed houses in Hampstead Garden Suburb, was among the pubs to open. Its survival and reopening in the face of a frighteningly long period of closure for the hospitality industry was all the more delightful because the Carlton had been demolished six years previously by property developers, just two days before Historic England were due to list it. A sustained local campaign emerged from the very literal ruins and Westminster's planning team responded robustly, obliging the developer to rebuild the pub from scratch. In a brilliant twist, the Carlton's locals had worked with Historic England prior to demolition, documenting and surveying the pub's fabric in case of foul play, so when the order to rebuild came the community was armed with a complete documentation, closing down any arguments about the impossibility of reconstruction. We weren't aware of the Carlton prior to its demolition, but it was clearly important to the people living and working around it, leading to an inspiringly vigorous campaign during which people and the built environment professions worked together to make something remarkable happen on a quiet street corner. We'll raise a glass to that.

Left: Simon Crubellier. Right: Steve Reed

Afterword
Phineas Harper

Mopping up too many G&Ts with a packet of Cheese and Onion, pub-going Londoners tend to tear their foil-lined crisp bags into silver platters for communal gorging. Like getting a round in, this modest gesture of collegiate generosity is central to the British pub experience. And yet we're doing it wrong. The 'platter method' might be comradely but, lacking edges, creates crumbs and chaos – prone to scattering its contents. Attempt the platter method in a pub garden and you risk a windy flurry snaffling your snacks. There is a better way; the North American 'bucket method' comprises scrunching up the bottom of your packet to form a squat tub. As the pile of crisps diminishes, more can be pushed up from beneath keeping a fresh supply within reach while reducing the chance of escapees.

However you tear your bagged snacks, it is the impulse of sociable sharing embodied in the gesture that matters – an impulse at the heart of London's pubs and this book. Pubs facilitate a remarkable timbre of shared civic life growing absent from wider London as privatisation and austerity chip away the possibility of public conviviality. Yet in pubs the divergent lives of diverse citizens barrel into each other – mutually enriched through sharing space, architecture and company. This book is a celebration of the shared cultural landscape of London's pubs and of sharing itself. So many people have shared time, wisdom and ingenuity in writing *Public House*. Many of their names follow in the subsequent pages but I want to thank the Open City Friends and supporters in particular whose generosity gave us the opportunity to create this publication in the first place. I also want to thank the editorial team of Cristina, David, Rosa, Rhea and Joy. This book is the work of many many hands but their boundless generosity and curiosity in the face of unending lockdowns has brought so much character and courage to its pages. *Public House* has been a remarkable journey taking us from the depths of medieval history to the farthest reaches of the city – thank you for sharing that adventure with us.

Cheers!

Contributors

Jennifer Lucy Allan is a writer, journalist and broadcaster with a PhD in foghorns. She has written on underground and experimental music for publications including the *Guardian*, the *Quietus*, and the *Wire*, and is a presenter on BBC Radio 3's *Late Junction*. She wrote and presented *Life, Death and the Foghorn* for BBC Radio 4 and co-runs the record labels Arc Light Editions and Good Energy. Her first book, *The Foghorn's Lament: The Disappearing Music of The Coast* is out now on White Rabbit Books.

Nana Biamah-Ofosu is an architect, researcher and writer practising in London. She combines practice with teaching at Kingston School of Art and the Architectural Association. Nana is a co-founder of Studio Nyali, a design research partnership, currently researching the compound house as a common typology on the African continent. Nana is a graduate of the New Architecture Writers programme.

Jessica Boak and Ray Bailey have been writing about pubs and beer since 2007. Their first book, *Brew Britannia: the strange rebirth of British beer,* was published in 2014, and a follow-up, *20th Century Pub*, in 2017. More of their writing can be found at www.boakandbailey.com.

Clare Cumberlidge, founding director of curatorial agency Clare Cumberlidge & Co, is interested in developing new models through which art and artists impact on everyday life. She has delivered pioneering cultural strategies, projects and programmes nationally and internationally. Clare initiated the Science Museum Art Commissioning programme, co-founded General Public Agency, an interdisciplinary agency delivering research and practice in the public realm, and Thirteen Ways, the curatorial and communications agency.

Ruth Ewan is a Scottish artist based in Glasgow who has worked with collaborators to create music projects, guided walks, radio programmes, design projects, education workshops and books building on her interests in creativity and social justice, and radical histories. She is represented by Rob Tuffnell gallery, Lambeth.

Paul Flynn is a journalist, editor and author of 25 years, with over 100 fashion magazine cover stories to his name. His first book, *Good As You*, a pop cultural history of British gay equality, was published by Ebury Press in 2017.

Laura C. Forster is a writer and historian based in London and Newcastle. She is a lecturer in modern British history at Durham University and is part of the editorial team at *History Workshop Online*.

Orit Gat is a writer living in London. She is a contributing editor at the *White Review* and has written about contemporary art, digital culture, and sports for a variety of magazines. She is currently working on her first book, *If Anything Happens*, a memoir that looks at football as a prism through which to explore questions about immigration, nationalism, race, gender, money, love, and the possibility of belonging.

Phineas Harper is chief executive of the charity Open City and an architecture critic. They have edited a number of books including *A People's History of Woodcraft Folk* and *Gross Ideas: Tales of Tomorrow's Architecture*, a compilation of science fiction stories exploring degrowth and urbanism.

Rupa Huq is MP for Ealing Central and Acton and author of numerous books including *Making Sense of Suburbia Through Popular Culture* (2013).

Sadiq Khan is Mayor of London and a former MP and human rights lawyer.

David Knight is a designer, strategist and author, and a founding co-director of DK-CM. He teaches postgraduate architectural design at the University of Brighton and was formerly a unit tutor at the Royal College of Art and Kingston University. He is a trustee of the Architecture Foundation and an external examiner at the Royal Institute of Technology in Stockholm, and is currently working on fiction exploring the birth of planning from popular and working class perspectives.

Alberte Lauridsen is a designer and co-founder of the feminist architecture collective, Edit whose work has been exhibited in the Oslo Architecture Triennale and Royal Academy of Arts.

Cristina Monteiro is an architect and author, and a founding co-director of DK-CM. In 2021 she was shortlisted for the Moira Gemmill Prize in recognition of excellence in design for women designers under 45. Cristina's work explores the complex history and ecology of places and she is a champion of equitable access to nature. She is currently developing a campaign to make cities wilder, more biodiverse places, writes a column for *the Architects' Journal* and is working on a TV script exploring spatial equality and representation.

Jonathan Moses is a writer and researcher. He holds a PhD in GeoHumanities from Royal Holloway University and an MA in Architectural History from the Bartlett School of Architecture. He writes on the politics of architectural design, pubs, ecology and phenomenology.

Rosa Nussbaum is the founder of Studio Christopher Victor, a graphic design practice based in London. With particular experience in book design and production, the studio works closely with clients to develop thoughtful and articulate responses to design briefs.

Lucinda Rogers works directly from life using ink, crayon and watercolour on paper. From a rooftop in

Spitalfields in 2001 she began to draw London and to record buildings and ways of life that are changing or disappearing, particularly in the East End. Her drawing of the Lord Nelson (p106) which was commissioned specially for this book is available as a limited edition risograph print raising funds for Open City's wider work.

Daniel Rosbottom is co-director of architecture practice DRDH, based in London and Antwerp, which he founded with David Howarth. The practice works internationally, with a particular focus on public and cultural buildings. He is Professor of Architecture at TU Delft and previously Head of Kingston University School of Architecture and Landscape, London.

Bernd Schmutz is an architect based in Berlin. Prior to forming his own practice he worked for eleven years at Caruso St John in London where he was responsible for a large range of projects in the UK, Germany, Netherlands, Belgium and Switzerland. He has taught at Kingston University and as guest professor at Leibniz University Hanover.

Neal Shasore is Head of School at the London School of Architecture. He is an architectural historian of Britain and its Empire in the 1920s and 1930s, and a trustee of the Twentieth Century Society and Architectural Heritage Fund. His first book, *Designs on Democracy: Architecture and the Public in Interwar London* is out in 2022, and he is working on his second, a new history of the RIBA's headquarters at 66 Portland Place.

Timothy Smith and Jonathan Taylor established Smith & Taylor Architects in 2010 specialising in progressive Classical architecture. Since 2011 they have led a classical postgraduate architecture studio at Kingston School of Art. Since 2017 they have taught on the Engelsberg Summer School in Classical Architecture and in 2021 they were the Harrison Visiting Critics in Classical Architecture at the University of Miami.

Bob Stanley is the author of *Yeah Yeah Yeah: The Story of Modern Pop* (2013), *Too Darn Hot* (forthcoming) and co-editor of *Excavate! The Wonderful and Frightening World of The Fall* (2021), and has written for *the Guardian, the Times, NME* and *the Face*. He is also a filmmaker, and founding member of the group Saint Etienne. He was Writer in Residence at the British Library in 2017.

Eleanor Suess is an artist, architect, and educator. She teaches architecture at Kingston School of Art and completed a PhD at Central Saint Martins. Eleanor's transdisciplinary art and architecture practice and writing have been exhibited and published internationally.

Isy Suttie is a comedian, writer and actress. Her BBC Radio 4 show *Pearl and Dave* won a Gold Sony Award in 2013, and her short stories have appeared in *A Love Letter To Europe* and *Dead Funny: Encore*. Her memoir

The Actual One was published in 2015, and her debut novel, *Jane Is Trying*, was published in Summer 2021.

Luke Turner is author of the critically-acclaimed memoir *Out of the Woods*, a reflection on sexuality, masculinity and the relationship between humans and nature. He has participated in collaborative exhibitions at the V&A, Hayward, and Serpentine Galleries. He is co-founder and editor of *the Quietus*, and writes for a variety of publications. He is currently writing a book on masculinity, sexuality and the second world war.

Lily Waite is a beer writer, photographer, and ceramicist. She is the founder of Queer Brewing, a brewery that raises money for LGBTQ+ charities and whose mission is to increase visibility and representation for LGBTQ+ people both around and outside of beer. Lily has won a number of writing awards, including UK Beer Writer of the Year, and was named *Imbibe* magazine's Trailblazer of the Year, both in 2020. She lives in London with her partner Charlotte, and her small dog Teddy.

Jaega Wise is head brewer at the Wild Card Brewery and a television and radio presenter. Having originally trained as an engineer, she was named Best Beer Broadcaster in 2020 and Brewer of the Year in 2018. She is currently a presenter for BBC Radio 4's *The Food Programme*.

Partners

ROCKET
PROPERTIES

Rocket creates bold, contemporary properties meeting the needs of London. They have led innovative developments across the city including creative work spaces in the east, homes in the city, and Linen Court, a mixed-use project in the tech hub of Old Street. Designed by Lifschutz Davidson Sandilands Architects, Linen Court is a distinguished, contemporary office building blending well with its surrounding architecture. At its base, the Three Crowns (p39), a historic corner pub, has been refurbished by Rocket including the restoration of its deep green glazed-tile facade. After removing the plywood facia sign installed in the 1980s the original 'BARCLAYS STOUT AND ALES' embossed tiles were exposed. These were largely intact with just some localised repairs needed. A local CAMRA representative expressed concern to the council Rocket were knocking down the pub. Rocket contacted the CAMRA representative to explain what they were actually doing and what had been discovered to huge satisfaction all round.

ELECTRIC STAR

Since opening the Star of Bethnal Green in 2008, Electric Star Pubs have been running inventive pubs all across London. They led the extensive rejuvenation of the Fellowship in Leyton discussed in Jessica Boak and Ray Bailey's essay (p72) and commissioned ZCD Architects to refurbish the Lord Napier in Hackney Wick (p190).

The Architectural Review

Scouring the globe for architecture that challenges and inspires, *the Architectural Review* is an international magazine publishing in London since 1896

Open City

Special Thanks

Dominik Arni, Tom Atkinson, Neil Bennett, Jon the Boatman, Tim Craft, Emma Crompton, Derek Colley, Caz Facey, Rob Fiehn, Kelly Foster, Rosie Gibbs-Stevenson, Paul Gorman, Brian Hand, Owen Hatherley, Joseph Henry, Ben James, Sam Jacob, Maddy Kessler, David Lawrence, Manon Mollard, Leo Pollak, Emily Post, James Ryan, Catherine Slessor, Maria Smith, Sumitra Upham, Rupesh Varsani, Manijeh Verghese, Cordula Weisser, Ellis Woodman. We would also like to thank the RIBA pictures library and curatorial team who have generously supported this book.

Open City Patrons and Best Friends

Ruth Allen, Christopher Attwood, Peter Barber, Patrick Bellew, Francis Botham, Patricia Brotherston, Paul Carpenter, Paul Carter, Martin Collins, John Curran, Claire Curtice, Anne-Marie Duchet, Peter Ellement, Maria Fitzgerald, Sara Habanananda, Meg Harper, Michael Johns, Crispin Kelly, Faaiza Lali, Alan Leibovitz, Chai Hong Lim, Janet Lowe, Andrew McManus, Michael Melnick, Farshid Moussavi, David Neilson, Rosa Nussbaum, Susanne Rauprich, Ludwig Ray, Jane Raybould, Helen Sanders, Maria Smith, Tom Smith, Mark Stadler, Paul Steeples, John Story, Jonathan Thompson, Gerrie van Noord, Carolyn Wagstaff, Yi Wen, Kevin Whale

The Londown Guests

Amanda Baillieu, Barnabas Calder, Ewa Effiom, Jonn Elledge, Edwin Heathcote, Dave Hill, Will Hurst, Will Ing, Ella Jessel, Hettie O'Brien, Oonagh Ryder, Oliver Wainwright, Lucy Watson

Borough Partners

Barking and Dagenham
Brent
Bromley
Camden
City of London
Ealing
Enfield
Hackney
Harrow
Hounslow
Islington
Kensington and Chelsea
Kingston upon Thames
Lambeth
Richmond upon Thames
Newham
Southwark
Sutton
Waltham Forest
Wandsworth
Westminster

Open City Champions

Allford Hall Monaghan Morris
Derwent
ING Media
London Property Alliance (WPA and CPA)
Rocket Properties

Open City Associates

Clarion Housing Association
Foster + Partners
Hawkins\Brown
Trowers and Hamlins

Open City Members

Almacantar
Baylight Properties
Haworth Tompkins
Peter Barber Architects

Programme Partners

British Land, Canary Wharf Group, The Design District, Grosvenor, The Howard de Walden Estate, John Lyon's Charity, Margaret Howell, National Education Union, Public Practice, Republic London, The Museum of London, Walmer Yard, Westminster

Accelerate Partners

Barking and Dagenham
Be First London
British Land
Central Saint Martins
ft'Work Trust
Precis Advisory
Southwark
The Bartlett School of Architecture, UCL

Accelerate Mentor Partners

Supporting Three Students
Alison Brooks Architects, Jamie Fobert Architects, Frame Projects, Stanton Williams

Supporting Two Students
Allford Hall Monaghan Morris, The Howard de Walden Estate

Supporting One Student
Archer + Braun, BDP, Carmody Groarke, Civic Engineers, Edwards, Jestico + Whiles, Gort Scott, Maccreanor Lavington, The Landscape Institute, Pollard Thomas, Surface Matter, We Made That, Whittaker Parsons

Media Partners

Dezeen, BBC London, The Architects' Journal, The Architectural Review

Open City is grateful for support from the Culture Recovery Fund from the Department of Culture, Media and Sport, and the London Community Response Fund from City Bridge Trust.

Acknowledgements

Credits

For Steve Barnes and in memory of J. R. 'Will' Williams

David and Cristina are grateful to the following authors whose prior published work on the pub has informed the writing of this book: Geoff Brandwood, Andrew Davison and Michael Slaughter, Mark Girouard, Maurice Gorham and Harding McGregor Dunnett, Paul Jennings, Ian Nairn, and Alan Reeve-Jones.

The origins of this book lie in a series of teaching and research projects undertaken at the Department of Architecture at Kingston School of Art Kingston University, and drawings from those projects appear throughout. In 2009-10 Adam Khan, David Knight and Bernd Schmutz taught a postgraduate programme at Kingston titled *Public House* from which this book takes its name and much editorial genesis. The students on that programme were: Yẹmí Àlàdérun, Dominik Arni, Ayna Azighali, Alexandra Bailey, Teena Cole, Stuart Darling, Carlos Dos Santos, Liidia Grinko, Timothy Hare, John Henden, Ming-Kun Huang, Alex Jenkins, Sharareh Khodabaksh, Sajeel Lotay, Rob McCarthy, Tobin McCloy, Dina Patel, Thomas Sellers, Mario Soustiel, Christopher Taylor, Rachel Vallance, Paolo Zambelli. Following the programmes, a school-wide project titled *The London Public House* sought to build an evidence base for a potential heritage listing. This was taught by David Knight, Cristina Monteiro, Daniel Rosbottom, Eleanor Suess, Timothy Smith and Jonathan Taylor and included every student studying in the department at the time.

Cover: A busy street scene outside Finch's pub, Portobello Road, 1960. Dave Bagnall Collection / Alamy Stock Photo

Endpapers: David Knight

The images on pages 17, 18 and 54 (bottom) were first published in *Victorian Pubs*, Mark Girouard, Studio Vista, London 1975

The illustrations on pages 21 and 162–163 were first published in *the Architectural Review*, June 1950 and later reproduced in *Inside the Pub*, Maurice Gorham and H. McG. Dunnett, The Architectural Press, London 1950

The menu on page 27 and 28–29 is part of the Miss Frank E. Buttolph Collection, a remarkable archive of more than 45,000 menus dating from the 1840s to the present day which is available to browse at menus.nypl.org

The lyric on page 63 is from the song *Where You're Meant To Be* by Aidan Moffat and is used with permission. www.whereyouremeanttobe.com

The explanatory diagrams on page 77 were first published in *The Guinness Book of Traditional Pub Games* by Arthur Taylor, Guinness 1992. For a detailed description of the rules of Old English Skittles turn to page 59 of that edition.

The images on pages 94–95 (p128–129) and 133 (p64–65) were first published in *Inside the Pub*, Maurice Gorham and H. McG. Dunnett, The Architectural Press, London 1950

The drawing accompanying the afterword was drawn by Alberte Lauridsen of architecture collective, Edit.

The poster on page 208 was published by the Temperance Council of the Christian Churches of England and Wales between 1925 and 1935. Courtesy Wellcome Collection

FREE HOUSES.

Colophon

Editors
Cristina Monteiro and David Knight

Design
Studio Christopher Victor

Copy Editor
Cecilia Tricker-Walsh

Editorial Assistants
Rhea Martin, Joy Mulandi

Production
&Printed / Studio Christopher Victor

Printing
Printed on Imitlin Neve and Nautilus 100% recycled paper by Kingsbury Press using colour profiles from colorlibrary.ch

First published in 2021 by Open City

Open City is a registered charity dedicated to making architecture and the urban landscape more open, accessible and equitable. Charity number 1072104. www.open-city.org.uk

Public House. A Cultural and Social History of the London Pub

Open City, David Knight, Cristina Monteiro and authors 2021

ISBN 978-1-9160169-2-7

Type
Set in Manuka (Klim Type Foundry, 2021) and Clarendon Graphic (Optimo, 2015).

The original design for Clarendon dates to 1845 and is widely credited to Robert Besley, a partner at the Fann Street Foundry whose workshop was located in a former brewery round the corner from where the Barbican Centre stands today. Clarendon proved so popular that it came to represent not one typeface but an entire genre. Signage in the Clarendon style soon graced the facades of many breweries and pubs across London and became synonymous with the commercial graphic vernacular of the late 19th century in Britain. It was likely this association that led Misha Black and Milner Gray to select Clarendon types for the comprehensive brand identity they created for Watneys brewery with the Design Research Unit in the 1950s, ensuring another generation of London pubs would adopt Clarendon as their own.

The characteristically bold, sturdy letterforms that make Clarendon so perfect for signage make it ill-suited for setting large quantities of text. François Rappo's take on the style for Optimo addressed this by adding light weights and italics without losing the overall character of Besley's original.

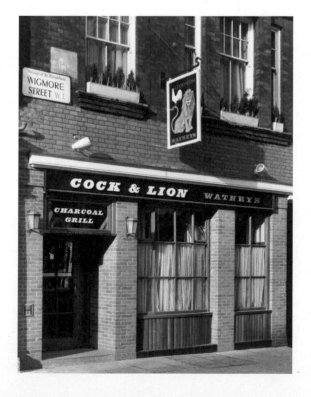

Left: Early Clarendon type from the *Fann Street Letter Foundry: A General Specimen of Printing Types*, Robert Besley & Co., *c*.1850. Courtesy St Bride Foundation

Right: Watneys signage at the Cock & Lion, 62 Wigmore Street, 1960 © John Maltby / RIBA Collections

OUTER LONDON SEE INSIDE FRONT COVER

ISLINGTON

CAMDEN

The Southampton Arms

The Hope and Anch

The Bill Murray

The Shakespeare's Head

The Wenl Th

The Belsey Trotwood

The Sutton Arms

The Glass Bar

The Fitzroy Tavern

The Little of Yorke

Ye Olde

The Jerusalem Tave

The Fox and Am

The Carlton Tavern

The Albany

The Social

The Viaduct Tavern

CIT

The Barley Mow

The Blue Posts

The French House

Mitre

Ye Olde Cheshire Cheese

City of Quebec

The Seven Stars

The Black Friar

WESTMINSTER

The Harp

The Lord Nelson

The Kenilworth Castle

The Hole in the Wall

The Lord Clyde

The Bride of Denmark

The Oak

HAMMER -SMITH

The Queens Arms

The Grenadier

AND

KENSINGTON

The Black Lion

FULHAM

AND

CHELSEA

The Anglesea Arms

Royal Vauxhall Tavern

The Atlas

The Cavendish Arms

The Joi Ar

The Duke's Head

The Coach and Horses

The Atlantic

WANDSWORTH

The Windmill

The Bedford Hotel

LAMBETH

The Kings Head